New Trends in

Dried Arrangements and Decorations

by the same author

The Art of Drying Plants and Flowers
A Handbook of Dried Arrangements and Decorations

Frontispiece: *Winter White*—see page 97

New Trends in
Dried Arrangements and Decorations

by Mabel Squires
photographs by Richard B. Green

M. BARROWS AND COMPANY, INC.
distributed by William Morrow & Co., Inc. · New York, 1967

Published simultaneously in Canada by George J. McLeod Limited, Toronto.

Printed in the United States of America.

Library of Congress Catalog Card Number 67-16369

to our daughter Joan

Acknowledgments

Grateful appreciation and sincere thank you to John T. Lawrence, for the idea of another book on dried plants; to Richard B. Green, who photographed the arrangements and whose appreciative response to my work shows in the pictures; and to my husband, for his patience, enthusiasm, and encouragement all along the way to completion of the book. His mechanical construction for some of the designs was invaluable.

Contents

Introduction

This is a book for anyone who wishes to have fun with dried plants and to enjoy long-lasting and appealing decorations. The ideas in its pages are designed to bring to your attention the newer trends in arranging and the innumerable uses of dried plants. Let us hope it will inspire you to create in the newer ways or to simulate some of the ideas described or shown in illustrations.

In our rapidly moving age of constant change, many forces are bringing about freedom of expression in all fields of art. This is definitely evident in the area of arranging, with a decided trend to a new concept. The present direction of all types of arranging—particularly with dried plants—is to design in a free, personal, creative manner. The arranger is at liberty to create as her artistic talent dictates.

New ideas often meet with opposition until they are understood and we grow accustomed to the changes. The easiest approach to an arrangement of dried plants is to go on repeating what has been done time and time again, but this is not half as stimulating as discovering new ideas to be used in the absorbing field of dried plants.

The dried arrangements of yesterday, with their limitations, are giving way to exciting, imaginative, and fascinating ones. The new designs are exciting in their use of all sorts of plant materials from near or far, imaginative in their personal creative interpretation, and fascinating in their freedom of design. The present trend opens avenues of expression more challenging than ever for the arranger to express herself.

The trend to the use of dried plants in the home is on the increase as homemakers recognize the great appeal of their natural qualities, which have artistic value far preferable to that of artificial materials. If you are one of the people who like to have something different in their homes, you can find many delightful ways to use dried plants for your decorations. There is no limit, once your enthusiasm is aroused, to the things you can do and the ways you can use dried plants.

Obviously, it is the aim of all women who make a home to have it as attractive as possible for the pleasure of their families, and to this end we all seek the stimulation of other people's ideas. A desire to share the fun and the joys that can be derived from drying and using plant materials led to this third book on my favorite subject. It is keyed to the American homemaker and concentrates on the newer trends for the artistic use of dried plants.

Anyone can dry plants: all you need is the desire to try. You will find that it is not difficult and that you have only to become familiar with the theory of all drying and to master a few basic techniques. The equipment and materials required for drying plants are neither hard to obtain nor costly. You may find that some are right in your kitchen cabinet or about the house. Instructions for the drying of plants are simplified and summarized for your ease of use in Chapter 9.

In the following pages you will find ways to use dried plants that you may never have thought of and decorative ideas to enrich your home and evoke the admiration of family and friends. The grouping of objects on a table, chest, or shelf will become far more artistic if you employ the principles of still life. For a wall of your home you can create a distinctive decoration with the use of collage techniques. Assemblage will prove an interesting field for experimentation. Abstract design may have to be quite fully explored to be appreciated. Dried plants also offer many varied and interesting possibilities for topiaries and for Christmas decorations. All of these areas are explored, explained, and illustrated.

The new trends in designing with dried plants are interpreted in the terms of the arranger, with the influences of trends in the other arts and the challenges of a free personal approach explained. Reasons are given for doing certain things in certain ways to achieve a definite result or effect. A bit of background information is included on each area as an aid to better understanding of the trend.

Some arrangers are terming all arrangements except those done in a modern manner as old-fashioned and are turning away from using dried plants in any traditional way. But it should be realized that there is ample room in our present way of thinking for all types of dried arrangements. There are many homes that will always require the charm and beauty of dried flowers in a traditional mass, in the rhythm of a line mass, or in the classic Japanese style. These types of arrangements have proven their worth by enduring for years and will go right on because they have much to offer for our uses today. They can easily be given a distinctive touch in today's manner of arranging. Although traditional and abstract are miles apart in concept and manner of expression, one type should not be considered superior or better than the other, for each has a place in our contemporary era.

For years the flower show did not permit dried plants to be included in the artistic exhibits. Today, due to the popular recognition of the decorative value and the artistic importance of dried plants, the up-to-date show will include classes requiring their use. The Standard Flower Show, presented so frequently all over the country by local groups under the requirements of National Council of State Garden Clubs, now offers an award for an outstanding exhibit in a section of artistic designs devoted to dried plants. In such classes are to be found many designs that show what a distinctive character this material has if it is used with artistry and creative ability. A visit to a show with such exhibits should be an inspiration to the homemaker and should give her ideas to carry away for the creation of designs of long-lasting charm for her home.

Who can predict what the trend in arranging will be in the next ten years? One can safely say that our present recognition of the many kinds of plants that can be dried is widening and that the development of better techniques for drying will lead us to use an even more diverse range of dried materials for artistic purposes than we do now. The designs we now think of as truly avant-garde may, in the years ahead, develop in many directions. Progress in any artistic area stimulates still more new trends. If one present trend in art is any indication, the change may be toward the realistic or representational, for many of our well-known contemporary artists—who for years have been concerned only with abstractions—are finding inspiration in the identifiable and realistic. But with "streamlining" affecting all facets of today's living, we probably will never be content to return to the trivialities and clutter of Victorian days, because our ideas and attitudes are now truly of the twentieth century. Who knows but you may be an influence on the trend that artistic designs of the future will follow?

Chapter One

Contemporary Arrangements of Dried Plants

Artistic arrangements of plant materials are a visual art form of our age. In the last decade, arranging gained enormous popularity, and the number of enthusiastic participants is ever increasing as people all over the country succumb to the fascination of this area of artistic expression. The potentials are more exciting than ever before, with the new-found freedom for personal creativity similar to that in other fields of art.

Anyone who arranges or who is interested in arranging will certainly have noticed that certain changes have occurred and that different styles are appearing in our present manner of arranging plants. The trend is given various names, but "contemporary" has been generally accepted to designate it.

Everyone who arranges today can be termed a contemporary arranger. Whether the artistic designs are done with a traditional or a modern concept, they are of our time. But not all contemporary arrangements are modern because many are based on styles that have been used for years. Truly contemporary arrangements have a distinctive, original quality which sets them apart as the results of our present attitudes and point of view.

TREND OF CONTEMPORARY ARRANGEMENTS

The twentieth-century arranger is no longer content to follow yesterday's ideas but branches out in new directions. This is particularly apparent with dried plants. Since we have learned to dry many more types and to retain dimensional form and color, the choice of plants is wide and diverse. Dried plants now comprise an important and valuable portion of the decorative material of our day. We have found that the inherent natural features of structure, color, and texture are satisfying and decorative qualities that artificial materials do not possess. Whatever the decor of your home, there are appropriate dried plants to bring charm and appeal to its rooms.

Contemporary dried arrangements show the awakening to the value of design, with decided emphasis on space and the important part it can contribute to an arrangement. Designs use lesser amounts of plants, and those that are used are selected with care and discrimination. Dried arrangements are not marked by a particular period, a certain design, or a special school. They have broken away from restrictions, arbitrary rules, and set patterns, allowing the arranger to express herself in the manner of our times.

The influences of the modern fine arts are evident in contemporary dried arrangements, and some of the most striking ideas are being accomplished in the modern or abstract manner. Abstract design is covered in a later chapter. We even find the influences of pop and op art showing up in some arrangements.

DESIGNING THE CONTEMPORARY DRIED ARRANGEMENT

The word arrangement primarily suggests an orderly placement of the various parts, with each arrangement being a personal expression and the recording of an idea. The manner in which the plants are used becomes the creator's means of communication. When an idea is executed with artistry in a well-developed plan, the arrangement definitely conveys its meaning as an arrangement of distinction to all who see it.

A bouquet of colorful dried plants will always give a certain charm and appeal to a room, but it cannot be termed an arrangement. An arrangement is a composition, and every composition should show design organization. If you ask what design is, the simplest answer would be this: the logical plan by which the plants are placed to express the idea. The bouquet of dried plants becomes a composition when the plants are organized according to a definite plan. It is particularly advantageous, because of the long-lasting qualities of dried plants, to take the time to attain a satisfying design. Glamorous plants will never disguise or cover up a poor design, while a good one will stand out even with the simplest of dried plants.

Creating a design in a dried arrangement is similar to the same process in any other expressive composition, such as a painting or a piece of sculpture, and the method is subject to certain principles. These are not laws or rules but time-honored fundamental truths. Such principles will in no way retard self-expression but when used as guides become an excellent means to develop a greater capacity for this expression.

There is a tendency on the part of some people to say that principles do not matter or that they are not important. There are others to whom arrangements of grace and charm come naturally. But, by its very nature, arranging demands an understanding of fundamentals before one can achieve the individuality for which we all strive.

Many words have been written and spoken about the principles that affect and control arranging. They are not as complex as they sound and are easily understood when actually put into practice. In creating any arrangement, you instinctively use certain principles as you arrange plants—and suddenly you realize that you have been using them all along in decorating your home.

When you make a dried arrangement, think in terms of building the plants into the desired design. Make its structure substantial, like that of any building, and establish a feeling of good balance with pleasing proportions and suitable size relationships of the component parts. Add a feeling of rhythm and some contrast and dominance to your design to achieve artistic quality. At the end of this chapter is a summary of design principles that apply to arranging.

TYPES OF CONTEMPORARY ARRANGEMENTS

The contemporary arrangements of dried plants will vary greatly according to personal concepts and individual furnishings. There are sheer joy and great satisfaction in creating individually for one's home. A person who delights in antiques will do her decorating in a period manner, while a world traveler may be interested in the Japanese manner to go with her Oriental pieces. Some people feel that only arrangements in a naturalistic manner are satisfying. Though the majority of homes may not be modern in all their furnishings, one may still find the modern style most satisfying. Each of these approaches can be termed an adventure to be explored for personal expression. The following material briefly discusses the general types of dried arrangements mentioned above.

CONTEMPORARY DRIED ARRANGEMENTS IN A PERIOD MANNER

Arrangements in a period manner can be a wonderful addition to carry out the atmosphere of furnishings of a former era. Such arrangements are usually thought of in mass because until comparatively recently decorative pieces were bouquets. The painting of the past can supply wonderful inspiration for this type of arranging with dried plants, but to follow the period exactly would be impractical. Designs are tempered to our way of thinking because today we expect something more, even in a design of period flavor.

Mass immediately calls to mind a number of plants assembled in a compact fashion. This is basically true, but the success of such designs depends upon their manner of composition. The trend is to lighten the mass and to give it an airy feeling in contrast to the crowded, buxom bouquet of

1

IN EARLY AMERICAN MANNER An antique grey ginger jar with blue markings on a teakwood stand holds an informal mass grouping of dried plants, suggestive of the manner in which our ancestors might have used them. The grouping uses the old-fashioned types of plants: amaranth as the dark outline spikes, grey artemisia to tone with the jar, honesty (lunaria) for its silvery sparkle, with yellow yarrow and zinnias for contrast.

the past. For the maximum effect, a mass should have a feeling of depth with some dimension and should never be either completely flat or filled to the point where it appears stuffed. Allow space for the form of each individual flower to be seen, especially after you have taken the trouble to retain its natural dimensional form during drying.

Do not consider such arrangements as formidable; in reality they are as easy as any other. You will enjoy dreaming up ideas to give them individual characters. After a bit of

2 IN A COLONIAL MANNER A diminutive mass grouping, 12″ overall dimensions, in the manner of Williamsburg. The lavender fan-shaped ceramic container suggests the shape of the design for the arrangement. The dried plants, chosen for their appropriate sizes and colors, are: larkspur buds for the outline, statice of white, rose, pink, lavender, and purple as the main material; pink and red roses and green foliage add the contrast needed.

3 IN A VICTORIAN MANNER A pair of hand-shaped chalk containers suggestive of Victorian sentiment holds small, compact mass designs. One was elevated on a small marble base and the designs were placed so as to unite the two hands. The plant materials are: statice in rose, lavender, and purple, roses of deep pink, and green perennial sweet-pea vine tendrils and foliage. The deeper shades of color stand out against the gold curtains.

practice you will be able to dry the right amounts and types of flowers and foliages to make these designs much more than bunches of dried plants. A colorful, well-done contemporary concept of an old design will always provide the special touch for a room, particularly in a container of, or similiar to those of, the period. Illustrations 2, "In a Colonial Manner," and 3, "In a Victorian Manner," are contemporary interpretations of designs with a period flavor. The pair of hands would be entirely compatible in a room of Victorian feeling, while the ginger jar arrangement is keyed to Early American furnishings in both its container and its plants.

CONTEMPORARY DRIED ARRANGEMENTS IN THE ORIENTAL MANNER

Today, in the U.S., there is great enthusiasm for and interest in things Oriental. Consider the influences of the Japanese on our architecture and gardens and the recognition afforded Japanese flower arrangement.

The Japanese equivalent of our term "flower arrangement" is Ikebana. With the many ardent devotees of Japanese styles in the numerous chapters of Ikebana International in our country, it is not strange to find the influences of their art quite evident in contemporary arranging.

4 IN THE ORIENTAL MANNER A free interpretation of the oriental manner using a dried branch of azalea to form a definite silhouette. Pink peonies stand out against the bronze container and bronze glycerinized peony foliage.

Ikebana is an art with a rich heritage of philosophy and symbolism. The Japanese schools of arranging are many and varied, each having its own styles and details. The teaching of one school does not necessarily apply to another school, so unless one studies extensively, it would be difficult to be conversant in all schools.

Japanese arrangements are generally based on three main lines, which are commonly called heaven, man, and earth. They are symbolic, and the angle of their placement in an arrangement is important to each school. The shape of designs is fundamentally triangular, with height and depth and the distinguishing feature of asymmetrical balance. Color is not of major importance, as it is in Occidental arrangements.

Much of the charm of these arrangements lies in their clearly etched silhouettes and the use of space. Each form stands out, with no profusion of material to detract from it. Dried plants are entirely adaptable to such designs, and well-chosen pieces can be done effectively in the Japanese manner to add a delightful touch to the contemporary home with Oriental pieces among its furnishings.

CONTEMPORARY DRIED ARRANGEMENTS IN A NATURALISTIC MANNER

There are people who condemn all arrangements that have a pronounced design in their composition and who go so far as to claim that the only satisfying ones are those in a naturalistic manner. Personally I consider this debatable. But because Nature gives many of her plants interesting ways of growing and because this growth can be made a dominant feature of a bouquet, the naturalistic arrangement is entirely possible with dried plants.

When you favor this type of arranging, watch plants as they grow to select for drying those that are of the most interest. Nature develops some of her plants in the most fascinating ways, with pleasing curve of branch, curl or twist of tendril, or detail of seed pod or case. Any one can be made a feature of an arrangement. Arrangements of this type may be satisfying and pleasing but are never as distinctive or as dramatic as those which show a planned design.

Illustration 5, "In a Naturalistic Manner," was made with pussy willows picked in early spring when the catkins were barely open, then dried as they grew naturally.

CONTEMPORARY DRIED ARRANGEMENTS IN A MODERN MANNER

The living space of the contemporary modern home is no longer the traditional environment of four walls. The old walls have given way to open-plan interiors, walls of glass to bring the outdoors inside, and movable partitions to open areas. In this concept of architecture, arrangements classified as modern are a decided complement to the functional decor of the home.

Modern arrangements are a product of our age and vary greatly, as do the types of modern furnishings. They show the influences of streamlining and functional emphasis of our times. Arrangements are thought of in terms of the space that will frame the completed composition and the mood of the room.

5 IN A NATURALISTIC MANNER *(above left)* Pussy-willow and birds to suggest spring. The branches, dried in their natural growth lines, form a pleasing informal design with a piece of grey-toned wood to unite them with the grey board. Blue birds contribute the right touch for a spring arrangement.

6 IN A CONTEMPORARY MANNER *(above right)* A piece of bamboo made into a container and an irregularly shaped board set the mood for a contemporary design. The large leaves of anthurium and the smaller ones of hosta form an interesting outline for the central grouping of angel's trumpet pods (datura). There is contrast of color and texture between the leaves of soft smoky grey-green and the tan prickly pods. An intriguingly shaped piece of tan kelp adds a note of distinction and interest.

The strong, clear lines of modern architecture are reflected in dried arrangements with stress placed on the values of design and strong silhouette. Vertical designs of height are popular and may have a decided upsweep in their lines.

Color schemes of modern interiors are chosen for bold contrast or in brilliant hues, making the soft tones of dried plants, by the very nature of their neutrality, a perfect note of accent. Many of the forms found in plants that grow in tropical regions are distinctively appropriate in modern interiors and have more impact than a bunch of dried flowers ever could.

Illustration 7 "Strictly Modern," is done without a container, in clear lines and neutral color. The somewhat unusual dried plants are composed in a bold, textured design with a strong silhouette. How well it would complement the plain walls and surfaces of a modern interior!

CONTEMPORARY DRIED ARRANGEMENTS IN THE HOME

As you enter a room, there is a certain stimulus in seeing an appropriate design placed on some article of the furnishings, becoming a thoughtfully conceived part of the over-all scheme. The arrangement creates a gracious and festive atmosphere and shows the homemaker's discriminating taste. The present trend is to keep the artistic touch always present with a more frequent use of long-lasting dried plants. They will glorify a room for long periods. Everyone responds to the charm and appeal of an appropriate dried arrangement on table, chest, or mantel, just as one does to fresh plants, and remarks, "Oh, how lovely." Once you realize how much satisfaction and

7 STRICTLY MODERN A design of clarity in a modern manner. Cycas, shaped before drying and clipped, forms a strong modern silhouette. Its green tone contrasts with two tan sea-grape leaves to carry the eye to the fascinating shape of a dried pandanus fruit. An unusual piece of wood completes the composition.

distinction dried plants offer in contrast to the artificial ones, your home need never be without the artistic touch of an arrangement.

HOUSE TOURS

The popularity of the garden-club home tour is spreading as a trend of the times. Each year garden groups all over the country select and decorate several homes in their community to be opened on a certain day or days for public viewing. The hundreds and even thousands who visit indicate a growing interest in seeing artistic arrangements in a home setting. An alert homemaker finds such a tour a wonderful opportunity to see how others express themselves and the present concepts in contemporary arrangements. The memory of a particular design in a certain setting will always linger to give fresh impetus for the embellishment of one's own home.

SUMMARY OF DESIGN PRINCIPLES THAT APPLY TO ARRANGEMENT

1. *Balance*—The visual stability achieved by the manner in which design elements are placed with relation to the design's imaginary or real axis.

2. *Proportion*—The visual relationship of one area to another in a design.

3. *Scale*—Relative size of one part of a design to the size of another part and to the place where it is to be used.

4. *Rhythm*—The sensation or feeling of movement in a design, created by choice and placement of design elements.

5. *Contrast*—The differences between certain of the design's elements that attract attention.

6. *Dominance*—The use of more of one thing than another in a design, or the emphasis of one feature such as line, texture, color.

Chapter Two

Still Life and Dried Plants

The trend in our contemporary world is to stress the importance of art. Great emphasis is placed on artistic expressions in home decor. Still life offers unlimited potentials to follow this trend. It can be a most interesting category with wonderful opportunities for the arranger.

Still-life compositions are known to have existed in the worlds of ancient Greece and Rome. Their favorites were cornucopias—horns of plenty strewing flowers, foliage, and fruit. Still life has been painted all through the history of art, each type reflecting the culture of the era. These paintings reached their peak in the rich and lush canvases of the great periods of Dutch and Flemish artists. Still lifes of various eras and artists are on view in our museums, including those of traditional, modern, and abstract painters.

Still life is an art form. Every artist, from beginners to those whose names are famous, uses still life to record personal impressions of groupings of familiar inanimate objects. The term differentiates this type of a painting from other types such as a landscape or a portrait.

The still life of the arranger is essentially similiar to that of the artist because of the necessity to exercise discrimination in choosing and composing objects to set a theme. But the arranger's still life should include some plant material, which is not always present in that of the painter.

STILL LIFE AND THE ARRANGER

Plant materials are the fundamental medium of the arranger. However, in the category of still life, the theme of the grouping is interpreted to a greater degree with other objects rather than by giving the primary importance to the plant material. The plants can be either fresh or dried, and the following discusses the use of dried ones.

There is a difference between an arrangement of dried plants, with one or two accessories, and a still life. In the latter, the objects are always plural and carry the theme more definitely than do the plants. In a dried arrangement the plants are the dominant portion and any objects are accessory to the over-all design.

The objects which have appeal to you for a still-life grouping may not have the same attraction to another. It would be extremely difficult to give an exact formula, as each composition is an individual interpretation. How can we say what a still life shall or must have in its compositon when it is an outlet of creative expression? The whole world of exciting things and wonderful plants is open to us.

Are you, as a homemaker, aware that you are continually arranging still-life compositions in your home? Do you realize that whenever you place objects on a table, desk, console, or mantel with a sense of selectivity and order you have created a still life? Once you become aware of the difference that selectivity and order can make, and of how much distinction selective grouping can add to each object, you will be inspired to experiment with this art form. Do not be afraid to try; the results may surprise you.

The objects and dried plants in a still-life composition are viewed as they actually are and can never be altered as they can be by the artist with a stroke of the brush. The arranger's still life is more fleeting than the artist's, as it is hardly ever recorded on canvas but is made for the immediate enjoyment of its aesthetic value; in fact, its parts are often disassembled and recomposed from a fresh point of view.

The spontaneity of any still life depends upon the selection and placement of its subject matter, namely objects—in this case, dried plants among them. Every object, no matter how familiar it may be, has an inherent personality. Its character may be strong and bold, as a formation of wood; dainty and fragile, as a piece of glass; or pert and saucy, as a figurine. Look at the objects about your home. How different are the characters of a plate, jug, book, candlestick, paperweight, box, shell and ash tray? For practice, think of the dried plants you could combine with one or more of these.

SOURCES OF OBJECTS

The sources of possible objects for a still life are everywhere. You could use a piece from a collection, either antique or modern, or something with purely sentimental meaning. The shelves in a closet may be hiding interesting possibilities. Who knows what you may find, if you look with an observant eye, to add interest to a still life?

8 SURPRISE The expression of the American-made pottery figure indicated the title of this still life. Its rough-textured finish and subtle color is repeated in the dried materials, which are pomegranates, mushroom, peppers, fungi, and ivy leaves. The slab of stones echoes the qualities and colors of the figure and plant materials. An interestingly shaped and toned piece of weathered wood adds a final touch to the still life on a simulated-stone wallpaper square.

On an outing or a trip certain things will strike your fancy and you will acquire them despite the fact that you know not how or when you will be able to use them. On a walk along the beach you just cannot resist picking up a beautiful shell or an attractive piece of wood. On a woodland picnic you find interesting seed pods to bring home. On your last trip the souvenir shop had such adorable figurines that you could not resist purchasing one. Objects collected in this fashion can be an exciting source of still-life material.

FORM, COLOR, TEXTURE OF OBJECTS

In choosing objects for a still life, consider their interest in terms of form, color and texture. Those of the same form or shape can be monotonous while variety in form and height add interest to a silhouette. A prominent object helps to develop the main theme if others are chosen to support it. Avoid using highly ornamental objects because they draw attention away from the total composition. Those of simple classic lines are most satisfying. Confusion and clutter will

9 ORIENTAL LACQUER Various pieces of black lacquer were chosen for this still life on a mahogany table. Ornamentation of the plate and boxes, typical of the Orient in its simplicity, required the selection of compatible plants. Two bowls, one inverted as a stand, hold three pale pink roses and their foliage, arranged in a triangular shape so often seen in oriental compositions. Their soft color and texture are a decided and pleasing contrast to the highly polished surface of the lacquer.

result from the use of too many objects, so let your good judgment determine what is appropriate in your home.

The repetition of a color in both objects and dried plants leads to a harmonious whole. In Illustration 8, "Surprise," the muted tone of the stone slab is repeated in the plants. You may prefer the excitement of contrast, as shown in Illustration 9, "Oriental Lacquer," where light pink in the roses stands out in contrast to the lacquer pieces. Experiment with light and dark values of color in objects and plants and discover how surprising the result may be.

Texture is the surface quality of any object or piece of plant material. A certain interplay of textures adds interest to still-life groupings. You can use the smooth texture of glass, the rough surface of stone or concrete, the soft quality of a fabric, or the prickly exterior of a seed pod. It is not necessary to include all of the above in a grouping; rather, you should use enough of a variety for a pleasing effect. Illustration 8, "Surprise," shows the roughness of stone and the coarseness in the pottery figurine and plant material contrasted with the smoothness of weathered wood.

ADVANTAGES OF DRIED PLANTS FOR STILL LIFE

Dried plants are an excellent choice for still life. They have many qualities to recommend them that are well worth investigating. One of the greatest points is that they remain charmingly fresh and appealing for long periods and do not require the frequent change of fresh plants. Water is not a requirement, and in many instances you need no container or mechanics. In Illustration 10, "Scales and Weights," the plants are merely laid on the scales.

10 SCALES AND WEIGHTS Old Fairbanks scales become the inspiration for a still life. Their red-brown is repeated in the color of the jug and both stand out when placed on the straw mats. The pheasant feathers add a different element and blend with both jug and dried plants. One can distinguish gourds, chestnut burrs, acorn nuts, and several green lemon (salal) leaves. Note the rhythm contributed by the placement of all the parts, particularly the weights, in the overall design.

Dried plants are economical for a still life because a few will suffice. Illustration 11, "Pearl," definitely shows that a few pieces create the right effect. Anyone can keep enough of a supply to use in different ways at different times.

OPPORTUNITIES FOR STILL LIFE IN THE HOME

Since this is not a book on interior decorating, the following will merely point out a few of the possibilities for still life with dried plants in the home.

A tabletop offers a golden opportunity to add an artistic quality to a room with a still-life grouping, in preference to using the surface as merely a spot to put things. What does your table have upon it? Are its objects composed in an appealing manner or is it cluttered with this and that?

The finish of a tabletop is your background and its length and width are your area for the composition. These dimensions are to be considered in choosing objects of appropriate scale, type, and interest. The purely conventional idea is to use a bud vase, an ash tray, and a box of matches as a grouping, but your setting can have a stamp of individuality with a more discriminating choice. The real point is the enjoyment that you and your friends will derive from seeing something of artistic quality. Are you making the most of this opportunity in your home?

With the increase of travel to the Orient many people include Oriental pieces in their furnishings. Tables in this style can hold pieces of jade, lacquer, or porcelain. An appropriate addition would be dried plants arranged in an Oriental manner in preference to a bouquet. Illustration 9, "Oriental Lacquer," is a suggestion for use of lacquer pieces in a still life with three dried roses with their own foliage.

A home in the country may favor Early American furnishings with a cobbler's bench as a table. A bouquet of dried flowers would be appropriate and in keeping with the objects suitable to such a bench. Illustration 10, "Scales and Weights," uses objects complementing rural decor.

11 PEARL Pearl oyster shells are the main interest of this still life. One is raised on a plate rack, the other inverted, to expose the luster and beauty of their pearly interior surfaces. Two fig shells and a pair of sand dollars lead the eye to the giant turban shell (green snail). The flowers which it holds were made by gluing the pearly disks of honesty (lunaria) to the lower scales of a cone, leaving the top scales exposed for contrast. The markings on an alphabet cone shell have the brown tone of the scales of the flowers.

In a home with a decided Victorian feeling, you find marble-topped tables with strange, cluttered assortments of interesting objects of the period. A small massed bouquet of deep color placed under a glass dome would be most appropriate to further the feeling.

In the contemporary home, shelves of various kinds are planned as part of many wall spaces and open ones offer the opportunity for a still life. How interesting an open shelf could be with the still life in Illustration 11, "Pearl."

A still life would provide a pleasing change of pace among the books on library shelves, on the shelf over the record player, or on a shelf in the playroom or the powder room. You can find other places for such compositions. Look about you and take the little extra time and effort to make your home more appealing by creating expressions in still life.

Chapter Three

Collage and Dried Plants

Collage is a delightful and interesting method of pictorial expression. Collages are not, as one might imagine or expect, pictures in the usual sense, such as an artist paints or draws. The medium for collage designs is actual objects, which offer wonderful opportunities to do something different and unusual, as they are personal expressions with no two ever alike. The results that one can achieve are amazing.

What does the word "collage" really mean? Its derivation is French and its meaning is "the state of being glued upon." Therefore, a collage is a picture made in whole or in part of anything that can be pasted, glued, or otherwise fastened to a firm surface. Actual objects are employed to express the creator's chosen idea or mood. The forms may be natural or adjusted for effect or symbolism.

In some respects, a collage is similar to a plaque. Plaques are designed to be purely decorative. A collage, though somewhat similar, is more pictorial and illustrative by nature, depicting a definite story or mood through the medium of dried plants along with other actual objects that have been found for design materials.

Collage is an art form of our century. About fifty years ago, Braque and Picasso began experimenting with collage elements in their paintings. The German artist Kurt Schwitters developed it extensively as his protest against manual dexterity in art. Today, there is great interest in artists' collages in exhibitions in major cities.

A new outlet is always welcome in the area of arranging dried plants. Collage opens another field for creativity. It is really exciting to see how interestingly dried plants combine with other objects for collage. Delightful ideas can be easily developed by an intelligent application of the design principles that every arranger knows. Anyone with creative ability can turn the making of collages into a most pleasurable hobby. The range of possibilities is enormous, with thousands of feasible compositions that may express a bit of fantasy, humor, a certain mood, or an artistic feeling for the materials.

It is the fashion in the contemporary decorating scheme to use pictures in groups on the walls of a room. Every homemaker is seeking something distinctive and individual to include in such groups. A collage would be a decidedly different addition. Anyone can fashion a collage, and if it shows some originality and a bit of ingenuity, it is certain to be the subject of conversation for those who enter the room.

DESIGNING OF COLLAGES

Any mystery which you may think surrounds a collage is easily dispelled when you realize that the design is an expression of your own reactions. Think of something, look at something, and what does it suggest? At first it may not call to

12 LURE OF THE SEA A collage to interpret the mystery of the sea using various sea plants and animal forms. The small buttons are mushroom coral, the larger pieces of coral are staghorn. The shells include angel's wings (large white pair), gingle, whelk, scallop, nautilus. The dark branchlike material is dried seaweed and the large center form a starfish.

mind anything important enough to inspire a collage, but after a little while an idea will develop. An animal, a figure, a tree, a flower, a leaf, or a color scheme may be the spark of an idea for a collage.

In Illustration 12, "Lure of the Sea," the starfish used as the dominating form was the inspiration for a collage of the sea. The background was painted in the blue and green of the ocean and the shells were placed in a rhythmic pattern to suggest waves. The tiny ceramic fish furthered the idea and helped to interpret the mood of the sea.

Collage technique has many variations. It can be completely flat, giving the effect of a painting, or it may have a photographic quality. Either of these effects is controlled by the type of material selected. A wide variety of plants are entirely suitable because many leaves, flowers, and seed pods become paper thin when dry.

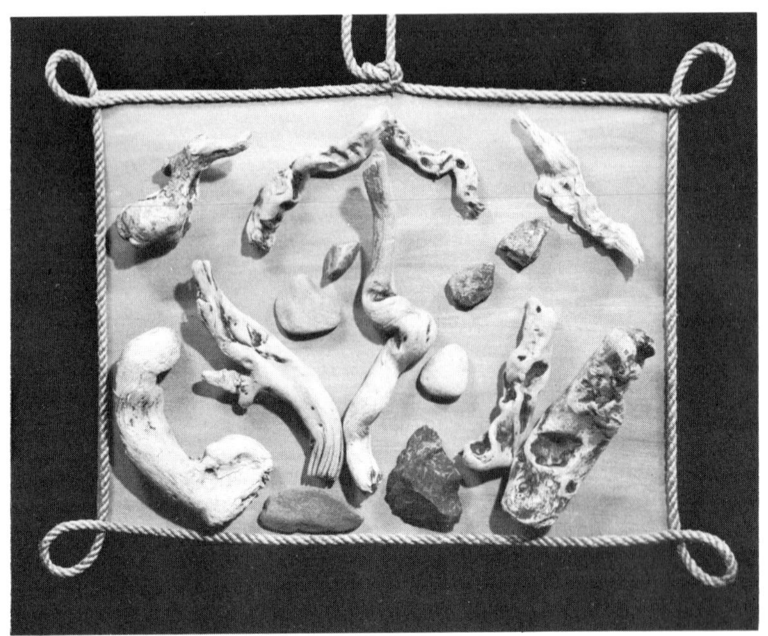

13 STICKS AND STONES Painting the background blue-green brought out the natural character and grain of the various pieces of weathered wood selected for this design. Each piece was chosen for its interesting shape, appropriate size, and tonal quality. The latter range from sun-bleached grey to deep brown. The stones include agates and were also chosen for the same qualities of interest, shape, and color. A length of hemp acts as a frame. How well this would complement a playroom, den, or library.

On the other hand, a collage may have a definite three-dimensional quality or sculptured effect through the use of objects with depth and dimension. The world of plants has a wonderful supply of fascinating shapes and sizes, varying in depth and dimension, such as seed pods, cones, branches, flowers, and foliage. The interesting sculptured character of pieces of weathered wood is used for the dimensional collage in Illustration 13, "Sticks and Stones."

There is much of real merit and beauty in the things we see each day. They are just waiting for you to discover and use them. With a bit of imagination anyone, either beginner or experienced, will find it exciting to discover artistic shapes and interesting patterns, textures, and colors in the things we handle daily as well as in the world of plants, which is full of such forms.

BACKGROUND

A collage requires some sort of a surface to provide a background upon which to mount the design materials. This surface should be firm and stiff enough to hold the materials securely. A thin or flexible surface may buckle with the weight of the design materials. The advised backgrounds are poster board, water-color board, canvas board, stretched canvas, masonite and plywood. You may find others equally satisfactory.

DESIGN MATERIALS

The variety of dried plants suitable for collage design material is wide and diverse. Any selection of size, shape, color, and texture of plants will depend largely upon a particular idea. There are sizes ranging from the large leaves of the big leaf maple or castor bean to the small dimensions of a single seed pod. The shapes are as varied, such as the spike of a mullein, the conical shape of a cone or a lotus pod, and the fascinating curve of locust or catalpa seed pods. Colors are many and allow you to select other values of color besides brown and tan. Textures also vary greatly, including, for example, the prickly castor bean pod, the rough poinciana pod, and the velvety-smooth pod of a wisteria.

Paper as a part of the design material can be an addition to dried plants when used cleverly. Construction paper and semitransparent tissue offer a wide range of wonderful colors, and Oriental papers are a varied source of material. Wallpapers are excellent design material for collage. When one is used to cover the background, it goes a long way toward setting the mood of an idea. In Illustration 14, "Dot and Dash," a wallpaper pattern was really the inspiration of the entire design.

Printed matter is another interesting source of ready-made design material and can be of any type that provides the desired subject matter. Textiles—with their wide range of pattern, texture, and color—may add the light touch collage needs.

14

DOT AND DASH A collage in the modern manner would be highly suitable for many of our present interiors. A textured and patterned wallpaper glued to a canvas serves as the background. Its light tone emphasizes the pattern worked out in dark dried plants. The dashes are senna pods, some split for flatness others cut to desired lengths. The dots are hickory nuts. It is framed with lightly waxed wood.

15
HARVEST IN THE AIR Simulated-stone wallpaper glued to a canvas board is the background of this collage. A small swag suggestive of fall uses dried grain, millet, leaves in autumn colors, pheasant feathers, with two dried mushrooms at the top. The small basket, split in two for this use, also suggests harvest as it spills its supply of various nuts. A giant olive-wood nutcracker from Spain adds a touch of fancy and provides balance for the two upper units. The frame is toned to the background. How appropriate to hang in your breakfast room or kitchen during the fall months.

Any object which suits the chosen idea can be used in a collage. In Illustration 15, "Harvest in the Air," a small basket was cut in half to fit the bas-relief idea. The sky is the limit, but keep in mind the adaptability of any object to both the idea and its practicality for securing to the background.

MAKING OF A COLLAGE

A great part of the fun of making a collage is finding the right plants for the objects you have chosen to carry out a particular idea. Not much practice or experience is required before you can develop a satisfying one. Those who have made plaques know how to apply the dried plants; but for those who have not done this type of ornamental work or for those who wish to explore collage technique in general, a little practical information will be helpful.

Once the design material is decided upon, actually putting it together is quite easy. It may be necessary to do a little rearranging of the pieces for a desired effect. The shape or line of a piece of plant material may determine how or where it can be used to the best advantage. Often, considerable shifting of pieces by trial and error before they are fixed in place is the most satisfying method.

It is easier to start a design by placing the larger pieces first and going on then to the smaller ones and lastly to the details. The success of a design depends upon the relationship of the solids—the dried plants and objects—and the voids—the open spaces. Collages offer an excellent opportunity to practice the principles of design in the way you balance a composition, the proportions you use, and the sizes you select. Some contrast is necessary to emphasize a dominant feature, with a feeling of rhythm to avoid monotony. These contrasts become evident by the way you arrange the design parts. Once the desired effect is achieved, you are ready to attach pieces to the background surface.

Remove each object and piece of plant material and place it face down on the worktable. Spread an adhesive on the back, making certain it goes right on that part of the piece which will be in contact with the background. A small piece may require only a drop or two of glue to adhere securely while a large one may need much more. On large pieces, spread the adhesive right to the edges to prevent their becoming loose later. If you are afraid you cannot remember the exact positions of pieces, make a slight mark on the background to guide you in their final placement. In an intricate design, you may find it advantageous to sketch it beforehand for correct positioning.

Once adhesive is applied, place the piece in its correct position on the background. If a design requires pieces to be close to one another, it is better to allow the first piece glued time enough to dry before continuing. The adhesive of your choice will have directions for its period of drying. In the use of thin design materials, as paper or pressed leaves, smooth the material gently as you place it, to avoid wrinkles or folds. In contrast, if the design material is thick or heavy, hold it in position for a few seconds to set. If the idea requires depth and one piece is to be placed upon another, allow time enough for the first piece to be firm before trying to secure any other upon it.

WORKING AIDS (TOOLS)

For the making of collage you will require a few simple aids in addition to the background and the design materials.

Adhesive: The best adhesive is a white (emulsion) glue, such as Elmer's or an equivalent. This type is easy to use and durable and, most important, transparent when it is dry. Library paste may lump and rubber cement may be visible through a design.

Brush: An artist-type brush is excellent to apply the adhesive to surfaces, and its size will depend upon the material. Never allow glue to dry on a brush but clean it immediately. Toothpicks or Q-tips are often helpful in applying adhesive to small pieces.

Tweezers: These are helpful in handling the small pieces of design materials.

Scissors: Several sizes may be needed for cutting clear, clean edges on various types of design materials. At times a razor blade or sharp knife may be useful.

Pencil and Ruler: Often they will be helpful in planning a design or proportioning space, so keep them handy.

Plastic Sheet: A practical idea; used as a cover for the working space, it will eliminate the tiresome task of cleaning a table-top when your work is finished.

IMAGINATIVE IDEAS

There are many other uses besides that of collage for the glue technique. Decorating objects with an accent of dried plants is an intriguing idea: it can add a certain something individual and it goes a long way toward enhancing an ordinary object. A complete list of things that could be attractively decorated with dried plants would be very long and diversified; the following are a few ideas to stimulate your imagination.

A hat or shoe box assumes glamour if it is covered with a gay paper and its lid is trimmed with some dried plants.

Plastic boxes, available in many kinds and sizes, can be given an elegant touch with dried plants.

A tin can becomes an interesting and attractive storage item if covered with Contact paper and trimmed with dried plants. Many food items come in cans with plastic lids that are just right for this treatment.

16 A TRIO OF IDEAS Interesting applications of collage techniques. *Top Left:* A glass apothecary jar offers a splendid opportunity for ornamentation with small colorful pieces of dried plants. *Top Right:* A Contact-covered coffee can is ornamented with small flower-shaped seed pods of miniature blue iris. Their dark brown is a pleasing contrast to the Contact pattern. *Bottom:* The lid of a small wooden box is more interesting adorned with dried plants. The large forms are coconut-flower calyx and other materials are acorns (nut and cap), pecan and hickory nuts, and undeveloped cones.

The jewel box or hand mirror on your dressing table will be individual with a personal touch of dried plants.

An apothecary jar is another suggestion for this type of ornamentation.

Baskets are popular as handbags and carryalls, and yours will stand out if it is personalized with some dried plants. It is best to choose these from the more durable or substantial types, as shown in Illustration 17, "Your Tote Basket."

Any one of these would be a charming idea to think of as a gift. You will be able to dream up many others, and undoubtedly you will find opportunities to use such gifts all through the year and especially at Christmas. An individual gift of this kind will be enjoyed long after the event or season has passed.

17 YOUR TOTE BASKET Select only the sturdier types of dried material. *Top:* The nature, size, and color of the basket indicated the use of heavy woody forms: cones of sitka spruce, pine, and hemlock. *Lower Right:* A smaller basket called for another design material. Long, narrow dark-brown senna pods connect the groups of sequoia and alder cones applied against glycerinized crab-apple leaves. *Lower Left:* Because of the color tones of the basket, the design uses a minimum of dried plants and includes glycerinized mahonia leaves, acorn nuts, and seed cases from a stalk of yucca.

Chapter Four

Assemblage and Dried Plants

Assemblage is recognized as one of the newer outlets for artistic expression and, though somewhat unorthodox, is practiced by many of the noted artists of our day. If we were to visit a major art exhibit in any part of our country, we would find that many of the exhibits had been done by this method in contrast to the other art forms.

Assemblage originated with the cubist painters of the early twentieth century as part of their revolt against stereotyped styles of painting. Just as the introduction of oil painting represented a desire on the part of the artists of the Renaissance for a new outlet of expression, so assemblage is characteristic of our times.

The word assemblage is almost self-explanatory: to bring together. An assemblage is an artistic work created by bringing together diverse elements, or parts thereof, which an artist feels can express an idea. The elements may be fastened together or merely placed side by side; juxtaposition is the term for placement of objects in an assemblage.

ASSEMBLAGE INFLUENCES ARRANGEMENT

For years we have used the traditional manner of placing dried plants in a container. The same design is often repeated until it becomes monotonous. Today, with the advent of new expression in all the visual arts, we find assemblage influencing arranging. The freedom characteristic of assemblage has influenced the arranger. She no longer feels that she must adhere to certain regulations but is at liberty to strike out in new ways and express her artistic abilities with whatever idea and material she pleases. It has given her an entirely new approach and opened a new concept of design.

WHAT ASSEMBLAGE OFFERS

Assemblage offers the arranger the opportunity to create her arrangements in a new, different and interesting manner, definitely of today. The difference between assemblage and other types of compositions is the highly varied challenge to the imagination, ingenuity, and techniques of the assembler. Assemblage also stimulates a person's ability to sense inherent artistic qualities in all sorts of objects we see or use daily. Your ability may allow you to grasp that certain quality in an item which the casual observer does not see until you make it apparent by use in a composition. There is fascination in the wide and diverse range of such compositions because objects formerly never considered appropriate are used with complete satisfaction and harmony. Test the pleasure to be derived from creating harmonious, interesting designs with various objects and dried plants. On the practical side, assemblage offers the opportunity to create definite effects with a minimum of dried plants.

ARTIST'S VERSUS ARRANGER'S ASSEMBLAGE

In many respects the assemblages of the artist and the arranger are similar, yet in other ways they differ widely. The arranger's assemblage will always include plant materials, while that of the artist hardly ever will. The concept of the arranger is to use this method to achieve individual and distinctive effects rather than the somewhat sordid, weird, and often ugly designs carried out by many artists. The arranger will mingle diverse elements, objects, and materials from everyday life with her dried plants but, by clever handling, create compositions of artistry and charm. In contrast, the artist frequently uses scrap or scavenger items.

ASSEMBLAGE IN A FLOWER SHOW

Assemblage is a familiar word in the vocabulary of flower shows, and classes for this type of composition will be included in the schedule for an up-to-date show. It is interesting to see the way in which people design their exhibits to answer the requirements set forth in the schedule. For example, if the class calls for a metal, a plastic, and a manmade object with plant materials, you would find each person's concept and choice of object entirely different. The viewing public is attracted to the stimulating and distinctive nature of such exhibits. And you really enjoy such exhibits when you have experimented yourself with such compositions. The displays take on an added interest because you can appreciate the creative work of another in this field of composition.

DESIGN PRINCIPLES APPLY

Every art form is developed through the use of fundamental principles; similarly, they apply to those of assemblage. The results will vary according to the way in which the individual uses such principles to organize her chosen design materials. Each one sees and responds differently to various items and objects. The same material will be handled entirely differently by two people. A variation in emphasis will always alter the resulting composition.

Assemblage, like all of the arranger's compositions, is created for use in a certain space with all of its parts being proportioned to it and to one another. Selection of parts for a composition is governed to a certain degree by the dimensions of the selected plant materials. You may use the reverse method to obtain a harmonious result by allowing the objects to control the choice of plants. Form and type of objects and plants are also important to the result.

Briefly let us consider some of the principles as used in the illustrations. Balance, as is well known, gives the feeling of stability to any design. In Illustration 18, "Del Norte 101," it is achieved by the placement of the upright piece of wood in relation to those in the lower portion of the composition. In Illustration 19, "Green Glass," the placement of the bottles in the over-all scheme gives balance to the other objects used.

Dominance implies more of some one thing. In Illustration 20, "Fall," the brilliance of the yellow and orange marigolds

18 DEL NORTE 101 Route 101 of the Pacific coast contributed the design material. Dramatically interesting pieces of weathered wood were assembled into a fantastic formation. The lower left suggests a duck rising from a pile of driftwood. The sun and the sea have given the wood and the kelp the consistency of stone and interesting markings with splotches of salty white substance. A piece of irregularly shaped bark is a suitable stand.

19

GREEN GLASS Articles of glass assembled on a stand of pressed cork. The dark green of pop and wine bottles and of the various-sized glass floats is lightened by the wheat, and rose-colored crests of cockscomb (celosia) are united to the bottles with leucothoe leaves. A length of rope twisted about the wine bottle carries the lightness through the composition to the wheat in the lower bottle.

20

FALL Man-made objects and dried plants. The interesting pattern of the Philippine basket blends with wheat, grasses, and millet emphasized with long dark pods of catalpa. Yellow and orange dominate in the massing of marigolds, gourds, and ears of corn from which pheasant feathers emerge as an individual touch.

dominates the tans of the grasses and baskets. In Illustration 21, "Naturally Sculptured," the wood suggestive of a head becomes the dominant item because of its unusual form. In Illustration 22, "Assemblage of Textures," the tall container is the first thing you see.

Rhythm is one of the most pleasing features of any composition. In Illustration 18, "Del Norte 101," the eye is carried through the design by the curving piece of kelp. In Illustration 19, "Green Glass," rhythm is evident in the placement of the various parts of the design, including the twisted piece of rope.

POSSIBILITIES IN DESIGN MATERIALS

The design materials accessible to the arranger for assemblages are many and varied and the choice of items to be combined with dried plants is infinite. One should never be at a loss for something with which to create a conversation piece for some place in a home, as on a table, mantel, or shelf. Each person will have her own way of designing her assemblage and of choosing her materials to carry out her idea. One may take the direct approach and use what is at hand. Another may discover important materials by accident, and still others will go to great lengths to seek the unusual.

No definite rule or formula can be stated for this type of composition. Selection of material is always personal. You may find that certain types of objects and dried plants are

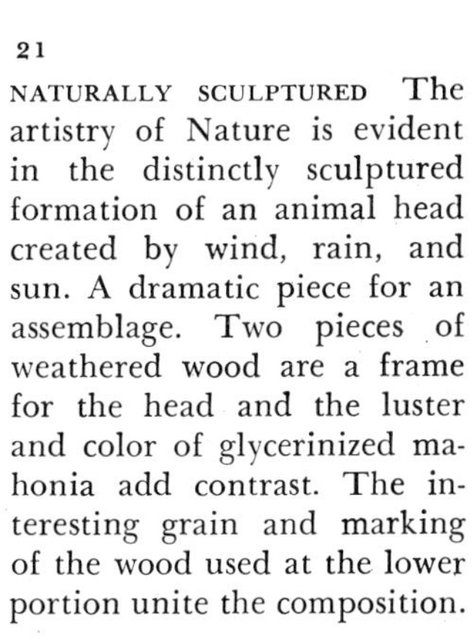

21

NATURALLY SCULPTURED The artistry of Nature is evident in the distinctly sculptured formation of an animal head created by wind, rain, and sun. A dramatic piece for an assemblage. Two pieces of weathered wood are a frame for the head and the luster and color of glycerinized mahonia add contrast. The interesting grain and marking of the wood used at the lower portion unite the composition.

22 AN ASSEMBLAGE OF TEXTURES
A ceramic, a basket, a metal, stone, and plant material are placed in juxtaposition. Each contributes its inherent texture to the whole composition, with shapes varied enough to form pleasing contrast. The ceramic container is green, the metal circle and disks are copper, the basket natural, the lava rock black, and the plant materials are brown stalks of mullein, tan aspedistra leaf, yellow gourd, and chartreuse Osage orange.

best in your home while those of entirely different character would be better suited to mine. It is fascinating to develop a distinctive assemblage by mingling objects from many orders of things. One could start with an item of glass or metal, something man-made, a figurine, or an interesting piece of a commercial or industrial material. Any selection of design materials—their number and kind—is dependent upon what the arranger feels is appropriate to express her idea. But the natural character and charm of dried plants will make her instinctively seek out items of an artistic quality in preference to the kind we find in some assemblages, such as parts of mannequins, neon lights, and bedsprings.

The use of an object in an unusual or unlikely way is intrinsic to assemblage. When used out of context, an object takes on a new meaning, just as words often do when removed from their original usage. The pop bottles in Illustration 19, "Green Glass," have an entirely different connotation by their association with the other parts of the assemblage. They no longer are commercial containers for a liquid but are thought of as artistic shapes and elements in the composition.

There are wonderful possibilities in objects of natural origin for use in assemblage composition. This does not mean only the interesting shapes and forms Nature provides for her plants but also the various forms Nature creates in areas other than her growing plants. The sea has many treasures in its animal and plant forms. Shells and coral are but two of the natural formations with fascinating shapes. Plants of the seas, such as seaweed and kelp, have intriguing shapes when dried. Do not overlook the interest to be provided by stones or rock formations in such compositions. The world is full of the most interesting things for your use.

Various pieces of wood have dramatic shapes to use as the features of an assemblage. If you are willing and your mind is receptive, the shape or form of a piece will have a strange way of suggesting a face, an animal, a bird, etc. Once you learn to encourage this train of thought, unpredictable things can happen, as the human mind tends to give every form a recognizable shape. Illustration 21, "Naturally Sculptured," is one of these shapes.

ASSEMBLAGE, A BROAD TERM

Assemblage, as used in the area of arranging, is a term broad and flexible enough to include many types of compositions in its classification. It can include compositions of various elements with plants, as previously discussed, or a composition of several units including plants which may or may not be fastened together. Assemblages with distinct sculptured effects are often made by fitting unusual pieces of plant materials together. An assemblage may be a free-standing unit. A mobile is a suspended assemblage of diverse elements with perfect balance that allows air currents to induce motion.

If we give a still broader meaning to the word, we could term all arrangements as being assemblages. This would seem a logical sequence, because in creating any arrangement we bring together various elements, such as container, stand, and plants, and often include accessories. The accepted meaning of flower arrangement is an artistic design of floral material in a container, while an assemblage designates a much more imaginative composition of diverse elements that may or may not touch each other.

In the broadest meaning of the term, we could say we have assemblages all through our homes. Look at the items on the vanity table top, the tools on the workbench, or the items on the pantry shelf. They do fit into the interpretation of elements placed in juxtaposition. The great difference in those of artistic nature is the discrimination in selection, with placement far less random and much more studied.

New methods of expression in any art are bound to meet with comment and criticism. But conformity to what has gone before is never as exciting or as stimulating as an adventure into a new field. Fruitful exploration in a new area is limited only by your own enthusiasm and imagination. Compositions created by assemblage are fun to do and offer a special kind of excitement and satisfaction in creating something that has not been done before and that is yours alone.

Chapter Five

Abstract Design and Dried Plants

Abstraction is a contemporary trend in art that causes much discussion of its pros and cons. Since we are living in a world where many of our attitudes have broken away from established traditions and conventions, it is not surprising to find abstract art influencing the field of flower arranging.

How do we define this trend in arranging? The dictionary defines abstraction in art as "using lines, shapes, colors, without reference to natural objects." With such a definition, we can conclude that although plant material is always used, since it is the medium of the arranger, it is employed as an element of the design but without regard for the manner in which it grew. The idea or feeling of the arranger is expressed by the way she manipulates the form, line, color, and texture of the dried plant material, abstracting all but that which she feels will truly state her idea.

ABSTRACT DESIGN AND THE ARRANGER

It would be difficult to know where or when this influence first appeared in arrangements, because by now it is generally apparent. It has a great similarity to the so-called modern manner of arranging. When the latter first appeared, it too was widely questioned and loudly decried. The boldness and severity of modern were a decided contrast to the traditional with which we were so familiar. As modern appeared in the architecture of the home, the need and the place for modern arrangements became apparent. Today with space so much a part of our lives, the need for spacious designs becomes apparent. Neither modern nor abstract design has replaced the traditional as many predicted, but each has added another dimension to arranging.

Arrangements designed in an abstract manner are a trend of this era. Their break with many of the traditions may shock some of the conventionalists, and others may loudly protest that the use of various materials is not flower arranging, but such designs cannot be ignored even if one does not favor them. They have definitely gained a place in our contemporary arranging. It is fairly safe to assume that we will be seeing them more frequently as people learn to appreciate their many potentials. This style has much to be explored in connection with dried plants.

CHARACTERISTICS OF ABSTRACT DESIGN

The traditional arrangement of dried plants with which we are so familiar will emphasize the representational association of plants. The dried plants will remind one of something previously seen or done, while the plants in an abstract design lose this identity and are considered only for their pure line, form, color, and texture.

One cannot say that there is a certain way or definite formula for composing dried plants in an abstract manner. But the switch of emphasis from traditionally decorative designs to the freedom of creative expression offers great possibilities to the arranger. The idea that promotes an abstract design and the directions which its interpretation may take are as infinite as our personalities. At first you may find that you have a preference for interpreting in a certain way, but as you continue and progress your whole concept may change. This is much of the fascination and the fun of the new freedom of personal expression.

Presently we are extremely conscious of space as we race through it to the moon. This consciousness is carried into all of our activities. The contemporary arranger is acquiring a different feeling for the use of space in her arrangements. Space is a most important part of designs of the abstract. Each form is a unit in the space of the design, and much of the success of this type of design depends upon the placement of the units. Because the shape of the space itself is such a vital part, we could almost term these designs of space. To this end all but the essential design material is eliminated by abstraction. The degree of elimination depends upon the idea, and the further the idea is taken from naturalistic reality, the more you have learned about the essentials of the idea.

When you design in this manner, you soon learn that restraint is an important factor in expressing ideas effectively and you also become far more selective and discriminating in what you choose to express a certain idea or mood. Each piece of a design's pattern is important for what it contributes and says in the finished whole. For example, in Illustration 23, "Butterfly," each unit of the design material was carefully chosen for the part it could play in carrying out the

23 BUTTERFLY The gauzy feeling of skeletonized cactus leaves suggestive of butterfly wings inspired the idea to simulate a butterfly with dried plants. Cattail and its foliage are the antennae and tail, a starfish the center body. The entire design is supported on an iron candle holder painted the tone of the plant material.

message of the title. You can easily realize that the removal of any piece would upset the whole scheme. If a leaf or a pod is sufficient to bring out the thought, one is not compelled to use more. An extra piece of plant material can stick out like a sore thumb and ruin the entire design.

The designs in the abstract manner will not follow the patterns we are so in the habit of seeing—such as crescent, Hogarth curve, etc.—but will be carried out in ideas which express our times with new, exciting, stimulating designs. Illustration 24, "Angles," is an example of the distinction and excitement of the abstract manner. Here a little plant material says a lot.

A freshness of concept is always stimulating. Never hesitate to put your ideas freely into being, no matter how far out they may seem. This may take courage, but it will be well worth the excitement and challenge of the adventure. Linear plant material, such as bamboo, was just such a challenge. Could five pieces varying in length be composed into a satisfying design? Their natural texture and finish were fascinating and their lack of curve was challenging. It was fun playing with the pieces until the design in Illustration 25, "Challenge," resulted.

Abstract designs may seem undisciplined and their freedom may appear to be incompatible with what we have learned to expect in arrangements. But if you really take time to observe and study some, you will find that they are very controlled and that they are disciplined by the principles common to

24

ANGLES Each part of the composition, including stand and container, is angular. The stand is a black triangle, containers of rough grey pottery have triangular shapes, one being placed on the other at a crossed angle. The cattails and their foliage further the idea by an angular placement in the upper container.

25 CHALLENGE The challenge of linear plant material—five varying lengths of bamboo. Many experiments with various positions and angles resulted in the design order illustrated here. Each piece of bamboo has its own place of importance. The placing of two to the left and two to the right of the central main piece provided satisfactory balance, space relationship, and a sense of movement.

26

ENTWINED CONSTRUCTION This preliminary photograph shows how the circular material is held in position. An appropriate length of bamboo in a cup needlepoint holder provides a firm foundation, allowing attachment of the vine at top and bottom. In the completed composition the bamboo will be entirely concealed by the design material. Notice how with some persuasion the top part of the vine is brought back of the bamboo, looped down, and the end positioned to carry the eye to the lower loop.

all art forms. Faulty balance, incorrect relationship of form, and extraneous materials are more obvious here than in other types of designs. If you train your eye, you will understand how others use these principles in their creation of this type of design. It is highly necessary to have a fundamental understanding of principles in order to achieve such designs.

Design in an abstract manner is often done on a large scale in order to have the necessary room for a sweep of line to soar for the interesting use of space. Again differentiating from the designs of former years, no special area of interest will be evident, as with a grouping of forms. Each piece is given its degree of interest and prominence, with rhythmic distribution allowing the eye to carry through all parts and over the whole.

27 ENTWINED Three bird of paradise (strelitzia) leaves, one placed directly above another, form a strong upward sweep accented by heads of yarrow in graduated sizes. The space surrounding the vertical design is encircled with the fantastically curved vine. Jagged pieces of amber glass tie the entire design to the cedar stand.

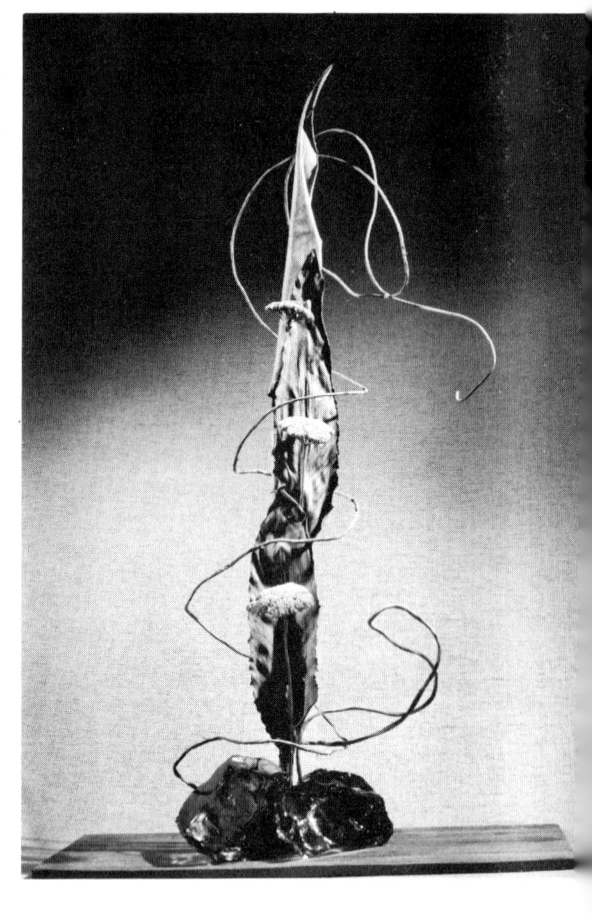

In the traditional arrangements of dried plants, a container is subordinate to the plants, while in an abstract arrangement a container is often dominant, prominent, or, on the contrary, eliminated entirely. In Illustration 24, "Angles," the container is a prominent part of the design, while in Illustration 27, "Entwined," none is visible. The mechanics of holding design materials in place must be done in a neat, tidy fashion, but it is not necessary to completely conceal them as we do in the traditional arrangements.

SUGGESTIONS OF MATERIALS FOR ABSTRACT DESIGNS

It is easy to find plant forms suitable to both drying and use in abstract design. For example, a cattail is a cylindrical form, a pomegranate is a round form of some depth, and a lotus pod has a conical form. Leaves vary greatly in line and shape, such as oval, oblong, and sword, to mention a few. Trees and shrubs have wonderful branches of great strength and line direction, and the tendrils of many vines are fascinating in line.

Plants that grow in the warmer portions of the country and are classed as tropical have dramatic shapes and lines. You could choose one of the various parts of the palm or the foliage of a warm-area plant, such as sea grape, dracaena, anthurium, etc. Cycas is easily coaxed into dramatic shapes. Yet

28
ANTLERS The interest of space is made prominent by its enclosure within two weathered branches. Their ascending curving lines simulate the title. A crest of red cockscomb (celosia) emphasizes the branches by its change of pace, and the twists in a dried hosta (funkia) leaf tie all to the cedar stand.

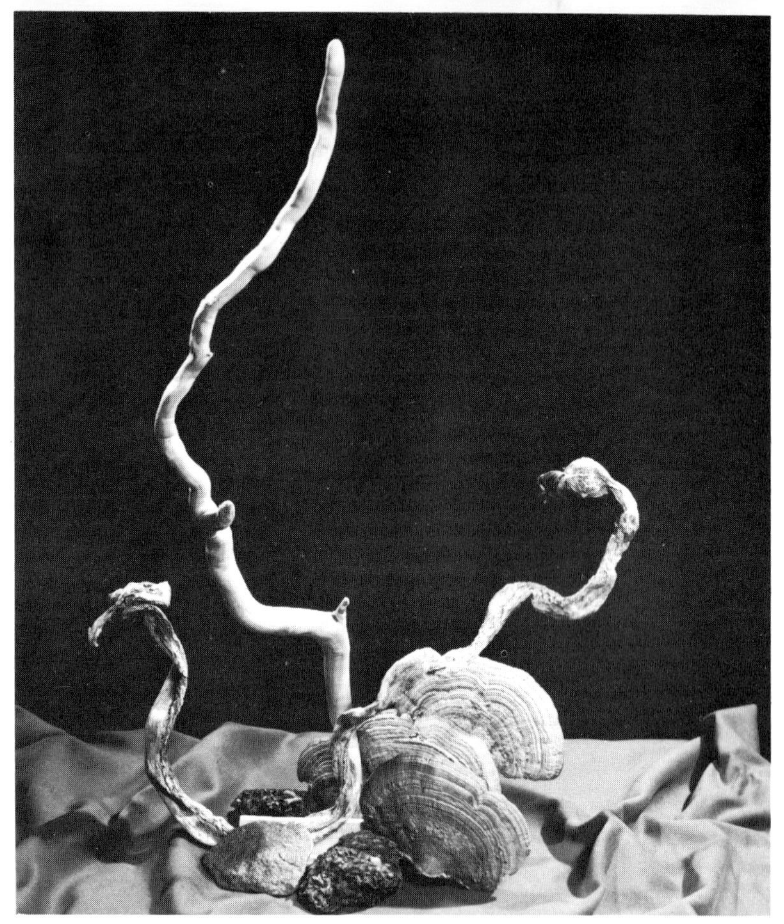

29 SERPENT A dramatic piece of kelp became the feature of the composition. Exposure to the elements has removed the moisture from this piece of seaweed and left it firm, of a warm tan color, with a shape suggestive of a serpent raising its ugly head to strike. A branch of manzanita and pieces of fungi were used to counterbalance the serpentine motion of the kelp. Three stones tie it to the writhing motion simulated by the folds in the fabric underneath.

with a seeing eye you can find dramatic pieces right in your own back yard. The point is to recognize the inherent character of a certain plant to be dried for use in designs of imagination and artistry.

You often find that the dried plants in an abstract arrangement are twisted, clipped, distorted, or otherwise adjusted to fit the purpose of an idea. This is acceptable and often advisable. But never alter the shape merely for the sake of changing it. Only adjust a dried plant when it will give a certain form or line that a definite idea requires. To achieve special effects, paint is sometimes applied to dried plants. This is permissible although not entirely desirable.

ABSTRACT DESIGN AS A CHALLENGE

Anyone can experience the fun of designing with dried plants in an abstract manner. Such designing is not restricted to the experienced or the expert but can be a real adventure to tempt the imagination and creative ability of every arranger. This does not mean to imply that everyone will be enthused in the adventure with such designs or can immediately create a masterpiece. But you will find that it is stimulating and informative to handle dried plants in this way. Through the experience, one gains a better understanding and appreciation of others' concepts presented in this manner.

Though the present freedom of expression allows a use of materials from a wide and diverse area for designs, these materials should never be ugly, weird, or repulsive, such as items in the category of scrap or scavenger. Personally, I do not feel that to place emphasis on light fixtures, curtain rods, or machine parts is in the area of arrangement. Anyone, especially a garden club member, who has an admiration and a certain reverence for the ingenious ways of Nature should strive to emphasize the plant's character of grace and charm instead of forcing the eye to items suitable for discard.

Arrangement of dried plants in an abstract manner may

YOU NAME IT Four pieces of weathered wood combine into an unusual container for a design in the abstract manner. The sweep of line in the fantastically shaped branches, one with backward and the other forward motion in its curves, carries the eye upward towards the space they enclose. Dried croton leaves contribute color to an otherwise neutral design.

not be true abstract art with the purely nonrecognizable forms of the artist, but it is the arranger's concept of a composition in this manner with her personal medium of expression—dried plants. She takes the forms, lines, colors, and textures that Nature has given the plant and, after drying them to retain maximum color and dimensional form, organizes them into meaningful and often symbolic compositions in the abstract manner. Since the true abstract is nonrepresentational, unless we wish to go in for the use of wire, pipe, scrap items, etc., the arranger's composition is really semiabstract, dictated by the quality inherent in the medium of plant material itself.

Chapter Six

Topiary Trees Made of Dried Plants

Topiary is a decorative idea that has captured the public fancy. Evidences of its popularity are noticed everywhere. This leads many people to assume that topiary is a brand-new idea, but like other things that are trends of the day it is a very old one that has been given a new dress to fit our contemporary decorative style.

What does the term topiary mean? According to the dictionary, topiary means "clipped or trimmed into (fantastic) shapes." In other words, we train or prune the natural shape of a tree or shrub into an unnatural, geometric, or ornamental shape. For indoor use, we construct artificially the forms of the trees, and many of the shapes used today are based on the clipped growing topiaries that were originated many years ago.

It is easy to find evidence of the topiary art practiced in ancient Egypt. The Romans developed it into a fine art in their gardens. Topiary was common in our gardens of Colonial times, and the shapes of the era can be seen in the box gardens at Mount Vernon, Virginia. For the past two hundred years, England has been the principal source of topiary inspiration. English gardens are world famous for trained plants, especially box, clipped into animal and geometric forms.

DECORATIVE TOPIARY

The present trend to using topiary as decoration in the home is most interesting because in an age when so much is quickly mass produced by machine, we delight in a decoration that is in direct contrast. It expresses individuality, requires handicraft, and has the one-of-a-kind charm not possible in an article made by an industrial machine.

As yet, no one has been able to duplicate the graceful and distinctive shapes Nature gives to her trees, but we do pretty well in fashioning fantastic topiary ones. We see them used everywhere as a smart decoration. The decorator finds them highly appropriate for hotel lobby, window display, and show, conference, and recreation room. A homemaker would be wise to realize their decorative value as a fashionable and individual touch for her home.

The ideas for such trees are endless. No two need be alike. The feeling, style, and covering of a topiary can be entirely traditional or as modern as you wish. Whichever approach you take, topiary trees by their very nature have classic charm and distinction, an air of dignity and good taste. Once your enthusiasm is aroused, ideas will flow in rapid succession. Your only limitations are the bounds of your imagination and ingenuity.

TOPIARY ALL YEAR

The topiary is considered by many people as appropriate for a decoration only at the Christmas season. There is no real reason for such limitation. Topiaries are appropriate for all times of the year, and suitable dried plants are easily found at any time. A tree of any color is possible, despite the prevalent use of tan and brown dried materials. Many of the latter are lovely, but to use only this type can become monotonous.

During spring, why not choose dried statice, in any one of its lovely colors, as a delightful covering for a tree? The addition of a tiny bird or several butterflies would be a realistic touch, as in Illustration 31, "Springtime." During

31 SPRINGTIME (*below left*) The feeling of spring is evident in this conical tree covered with purple statice and accented with pink rosebuds and butterflies. GLOWING ORANGE (*below right*) Strawflowers are a delightful covering for a ball-shaped tree. Five dozen orange flowers cover the 8″ ball on an 18″ dowel. The gleam of a large orange satin bow enhances the tree with flowing color.

33 A SYMPHONY OF TONES *(above left)* An inverted gilded glass is the stand for a conical tree in soft tones. Its interest lies in the happy combination of tones, textures, and shapes of plants. Tan safflowers were used for their prickly-textured round forms and the dashes of orange in the tan which lighten the effect; yarrow for its golden tone and dull texture; melaleuca pods for their gloss and curving shapes; flower-shaped seed pods of columbine (aquilegia) for their green tone; cones and eucalyptus pods for their tones of brown.

34 LITTLE JEWEL *(above right)* A white ceramic pot holds a dainty tree of pastel dried plants. The overall height of 12" calls for the smaller types to keep scale relationships. They include white, pink, and lavender statice, yarrow for a yellow tone, individual florets of blue delphinium, and small sections of red cockscomb (celosia). Siberian iris pods create spikes for a more interesting silhouette. A rainbow ribbon winds around the dowel and ends in a bow.

summer, when the strawflowers come into bloom, think about using one of their colors—such as rose, pink, red, yellow, or orange—to cover a tree. In the fall there are many interesting things for a tree covering. You will find that dried goldenrod or yarrow will make a delightful tree. Or if you wish to do the unusual, try a tree of seed pods, dried mushrooms, and chestnuts. Trees for Christmas are discussed later in this chapter.

USES OF TOPIARY

The functional interiors of contemporary homes offer many places entirely suitable for one of these little gems of artistry. A tree of this kind is free-standing and attractive from any vantage point. One would look well placed against a plain wall, so prevalent in the contemporary home, and the shape of a tree would be intriguing silhouetted in a picture window. An interesting tree on a coffee table will always cause conversation. You may do one for the entry-hall table, the radio, hi-fi, or television console, or a pair for the mantel. One or two are a distinctive touch on a dining-room table or sideboard. A topiary tree of dainty proportions would be charming in a bedroom.

Like any other decorative touch in a room, the tree should be suited to the furnishings in style, shape, and size. The proportions should be considered in relation to the piece of furniture on which the tree is to be placed. If it is too large, it will be overpowering, and if it is too small, it will be insignificant. In certain places a conical- or pyramid-shaped tree will look best, in preference to a ball-shaped one, or vice versa. Select the type your taste tells you is best for your room.

The shape of a topiary is usually based on a geometric form,

35 ITEMS FOR THE MAKING OF TREES An assortment of Styrofoam shapes used in making topiary trees. Flowerpots, both upright and inverted, show the positioning of dowels as standards or trunks for the tree shapes.

such as a ball, cone, pyramid, triangle, or combination of these. The espalier is another possibility. The following suggests the basic construction of each type of tree, to be decorated as you please.

STRUCTURES FOR TREES

Styrofoam is a plastic material that has become the popular favorite for the structural element of a topiary. It has many advantages: it is strong yet light, is clean to handle, works well with many types of dried plants, is inexpensive, and is available in various shapes and sizes. There are balls from one inch to eight inches, cones from five to eighteen inches, and pyramids from six to twelve inches. If a special shape is desired, Styrofoam is available in large sheets, twelve inches by eighteen inches, in various thicknesses, and it is easily cut with a sharp knife into the shapes you want.

Plywood is another material from which to construct a frame of a tree. It is the most satisfactory for a triangular tree covered with the heavier types of dried plants. (See cone trees for Christmas later in this chapter.)

Some people use cardboard or layers of newspapers to construct the frame of a conical tree, but Styrofoam seems the most practical answer because at small cost you have a form all ready to be covered.

BALL SHAPE

The ball is the prevalent shape for a topiary. Comparatively, it is the easiest and simplest to make, particularly for your first attempt. Let us start with a simple item, the familiar clay flowerpot, and use it as the base for a tree. These pots are practical, being available in various sizes, inexpensive, usable upright or inverted, and easily painted to harmonize with the color scheme of the tree. If you do not wish to use a clay one, there are many other kinds of flowerpots to be found.

There is nothing better as a trunk to support the ball shape than a half-inch dowel stick. The length depends upon the size of the ball; eighteen inches is a good proportion for a six- or seven-inch flowerpot. To keep the dowel erect inside the flowerpot, you will need something for an anchoring medium, such as plaster of Paris or paraffin. Place the dowel in the correct position while the anchoring medium is pliable, and place enough of it in the pot to hold the dowel firmly. Wait until it is firmly set before impaling the ball on the upper end of the dowel. Now you are ready for the decorative covering and any other ornamentation. Illustration 39, "Accent on Silver," shows an average-sized ball-shaped tree constructed as described, with a flowerpot base and dowel trunk.

Other articles besides a flowerpot are suitable for the base of a ball-shaped tree—for example, a circle of wood with a hole in the center to anchor the dowel, a ceramic container, a freezer box, or even a tin can. With all except the wood, you need an anchoring medium, and the box or can should be covered or painted in some appropriate way.

A tree may consist of more than one ball shape. Many lovely ones are made with two or three ball formations, and according to personal taste they may be all alike in size and covering or varied. In the use of several sizes of balls for a tree, it is most satisfactory if the smallest one is at the top and the largest at the bottom, as in Illustration 38, "Trio."

CONE AND PYRAMID

A cone- or pyramid-shaped topiary can be used with or without a base. An inexpensive footed glass will make an excellent base for one of these shapes. When inverted, the flat undersurface of the foot can be glued to the bottom of the cone or pyramid. Either a flowerpot or a circle of wood is appropriate, too, but you will find that the cones or pyramids are as effective without bases of their own or set upon circles of fabric or teakwood stands.

The over-all appearance of such a shape is most attractive if the covering is attached in a set pattern. There is a particular appeal if the design material flows in a rhythmic way *around* the cone or pyramid. The same feeling can also be achieved by ornamenting the all-over covering with a definite design of some additional contrasting material.

TRIANGULAR SHAPE

The flat triangle is another of the possible geometric forms to be used for a topiary. The three sides of the triangle may be equal or the horizontal bottom side may be shorter than the other two. Personally, I feel that the narrow-based proportions give a far more pleasing result. A form for a tree of this shape is easily cut from foam or plywood. It will need a base and a standard to keep it erect, and these are not difficult to make. Remember that when you do make a form of any kind, it can always be kept and given fresh adornment. You will be amazed at the different new coverings you can make.

The lighter types of dried plants are best for a Styrofoam triangle, with the standard and base also cut from foam. For the heavier types of dried plants, such as seed pods and cones, plywood is far better and the base can be a block of wood and the standard a dowel. Description of this type of tree is given in the section on Christmas trees.

ESPALIER SHAPE

Espalier is another shape for a topiary. It is derived from the garden trellis or frame upon which fruit trees are trained. This idea is easily developed into a delightful tree. It is unusual and has not often been used as the inspiration for a decorative topiary.

For this, you also need to make a frame, but this is a simple matter. Start with a substantial square dowel of one-quarter to three-eighths of an inch as the main trunk and standard. The length will depend upon the height you wish. Anchor the

36

IVY AND ROSES Espalier, a tree form of charm and individuality, made by attaching ivy leaves with glue to a dowel wood frame mounted on a crossed wood stand. Roses add contrast and emphasize the espalier shape.

dowel in a square or round piece of wood. The horizontal branches come next. They are square dowels, of graduated lengths, attached at intervals at right angles to the trunk, so the ends form tapered sides for the tree. Watch for good proportion and balance as you attach the widest piece at the lower part of the vertical trunk, and let the pieces grow narrower as they go upward. Three or four horizontals are ample for a tree of average size. When the frame is complete, it may remain natural, be painted, or be covered with corsage tape.

The decorative covering should be selected from dried plant materials of appropriate size, such as small cones, seed pods, flowers, and leaves. Many of the smaller leaves dry well; ivy and oval eucalyptus are but two possibilities. One suggestion is to cover the frame with small leaves, each attached to the frame with a few drops of glue. Then at strategic points place groupings of other dried material to emphasize the espalier shape. You will find that keeping an espalier somewhat in the garden mood makes it a most satisfying tree for a playroom, library, or possibly a kitchen.

DECORATIVE COVERING OF STYROFOAM TREES

For the covering you can select from a wide range of plants. Each tree is an individual creation, so select the covering to suit your taste and really enjoy it. The mood of a tree is set by its covering. If you wish it to be soft and fluffy, select this type of material; if you prefer a more tailored effect, choose the sturdier types of dried plants.

The manner in which the covering is attached to the form of a tree will depend largely upon the nature of the dried material. Some types require only the end of a stem to be sharpened before it is inserted into the foam. Sometimes the foam seems to have a sort of waxy film and it is difficult to insert the material, so make a tiny hole in the foam with a toothpick and your dried plant stem will easily slip into it. Another type of material may need a bit of fine wire, a straight pin, or a toothpick to attach it securely. Still others remain firm with a drop of glue. After a few experiments, you will become resourceful in developing your own clever ways to attach decorative coverings.

Start the covering wherever you wish, but always continue it until the shape is completely and evenly covered. Be careful to retain the original shape as you cover. This even silhouette is a large part of the charm of any topiary, particularly the ball-shaped one. Keep in mind that the covering always increases the size; if you use a material of some depth, you may find that you have doubled the tree's original size when you have finished it. If the final result can be improved with adjustment of size or shape of the dried material, don't hesitate to cut it. This applies to the covering of all topiary trees.

TOPIARY FOR CHRISTMAS

For Christmas, you can really let your imagination soar in thinking up ideas for trees. When you make a topiary for your home at this season, do it with a flourish that is distinctively personal, with your mark of individuality. Trees may be entirely traditional or fantastically modern, depending upon the atmosphere of your home. The trend at Christmas is, of course, to do trees of a natural material in preference to trees with other types of decorative coverings, and dried plants, being so close to Nature, seem a most fitting choice for a topiary to complement the traditional evergreen Christmas tree.

CONE TOPIARY

One of the first dried plant materials we think of at Christmas is the cone. It is a traditional dried material, and the wide variety of sizes, shapes, and kinds that develop on the evergreens is fantastic. (Summer is the time to start collecting cones for Christmas.) They are extremely versatile and will fit into many different ideas for decorative trees. The values of tan and brown, natural to a cone when it is dry, are lovely and trees of these colors can be decided accents in homes

37 BEAUTY IN BROWN *(above left)* A collection of cones placed in a definite pattern on a triangular piece of plywood forms an interesting tree. There are cones of scotch, white, ponderosa, pitch, and pinyon pine; Douglas fir, giant sequoia, cedar (deodar), and hemlock. Individual scales of a fir cone edge the triangle. Large cones are used at the base, including one of the interesting knob-pine cones. 38 TRIO *(above right)* A three-ball topiary covered with hemlock cones and completed with perky gold-toned velvet ribbon bows was made as described in the text.

where there are various types of contemporary furnishings. But cones are entirely adaptable to artificial coloring, too, and a tree may be any color you wish for an interior, from metallic colors to those completely unexpected but still charming, such as sky blue or rosy pink.

A personal favorite of mine appears in Illustration 37, "Beauty in Brown." It began with an interesting collection of cones and the cutting of a plywood triangle to be used as the form. The form has a twelve-inch base and twenty-two-inch sides. It was mounted on a short fat dowel set in a circle of wood, giving a height of thirty inches. To accommodate the design, which was planned for the wide variety of cones we had, the tree was intentionally made this large size. A frame of this kind is well worth while, though it does take a bit of time to make.

In line with a definite design idea, each of the cones to be used was selected for its size, shape, and texture. The individual nature of each one was to contribute in a measure to the completed pattern. The entire pattern of the design was laid out on the plywood triangle before each cone was attached with glue. You will notice that the larger cones are placed at the lower portion to provide stability and balance and that the cones decrease in size as the pattern progresses upward. To vary the pattern, some cones were placed in silhouette and others were reversed to expose their roselike undersurfaces. (The caption on Illustration 37 gives the names of the cone varieties used.) The harsh edge of the triangular frame was relieved in a pleasing way by the use of individual scales removed from a fir cone. (Fir cones come apart easily, as they shatter to expel their seeds.) When the design was completed, the tonal values in the cones contrasted attractively with the lightness of the unfinished plywood.

The graduated three-ball tree in Illustration 38, "Trio," shows quite a different use of cones for a Christmas topiary. Its construction is the same as that for the single-ball tree described before, with a dowel anchored in a plastic flowerpot with plaster of Paris. Since we had previously collected a bagful of various sizes of hemlock cones, this one variety was used for the decorative covering of all three balls. The smallest cones cover the top ball, and the sizes are graduated to the largest ones on the bottom ball. Just a flick of gold spray gave a glittering highlight to the brown of each cone on the completed tree. Bows of gold velvet ribbon added the final touch.

ACCENT ON SILVER Form and texture are stressed in this well shaped tree by the covering of silvered sweet-gum balls interspaced with glittered toothpicks. Silver ribbon in a many-looped bow and silvered flowerpot continue the theme of the title.

METALLIC TOPIARY

Stunning effects can be created on a well-constructed topiary by the application of a metallic paint. A tree of this nature is often more satisfying in a room than an untreated one. If the living room has rose or blue tones in its furnishings, a silver topiary would be entirely harmonious; if green or blue-green predominate, a copper-colored topiary might be attractive; or with tones of brown or yellow, perhaps a gold topiary.

Metallic paints are available in spray cans in these silver, copper, and gold colors. Aluminum gives a lustrous silver, and dull gold is softer and more pleasing than a bright and shiny paint. Spray cans are the most convenient to use, for with a mere push of the button the paint is easily released and controlled.

The decorative covering of the topiary in Illustration 39, "Accent on Silver," is composed of the spiny balls of sweet gum (liquid-amber). The flowerpot, dowel, and balls were sprayed with silver (aluminum). Toothpicks, previously silvered and lavishly glittered, were used at intervals to relieve the roundness of the form and add a starry sparkle. A silver bow completes a stunning decorative topiary.

WHITE TOPIARY

The frosty look of an all-white topiary is always attractive and effective, with the whiteness appropriately symbolic of the snow we associate with the Christmas season. Such a tree can bring a light touch to a dark corner or, because of its lack of color, be just right for a room of brilliant hue. A white topiary is especially attractive for use on a dining table.

A white tree is excellent for using dried plant material that may have lost color but whose shape is still good. If you do follow this suggestion, construct the tree in its entirety before you apply the paint. Spraying with a pressure can is the best and quickest method to assure an even covering. A white tree is charming with a gold or silver ribbon, and if you give the tree a lavish dose of glitter, it really turns into a glamorous piece. Glittering must be done while the paint is wet. To be sure the glitter sticks to all parts of the tree, I like to spray the paint with one hand and sprinkle on the glitter with the other hand at the same time.

Artificial snow, also available in pressure cans, is another covering for a white tree. You will hardly recognize the snow-covered tree as the one with which you started. Color can always be added, if you wish, with the addition of ornaments or ribbon.

If you are a person who likes to do the daring, try a black and white combination. Paint the base and trunk of a topiary a shiny black and the decorative covering a dull white. Add cerise or chartreuse ribbon bows for color, and you have a fanciful modern topiary. Not every home can use this type of decoration, but in many modern interiors it would be a decided asset.

Any homemaker will have accomplished something special for her home at Christmas by making several of these little trees. And remember that they also make delightful gifts.

Chapter Seven

New Variations for Christmas Decorations with Dried Plants

Christmas has various meanings and associations to different people. It may be the star in the window, the wreath on the door, or the crèche under the tree that has special significance to you. Each year we pay homage to our past as we enjoy the happy associations of these traditional decorations. No Christmas would be complete without one or more of them. Yet to move with the times we often give these decorations a new twist.

Christmas calls for decorations not in one or two places but all through the house. Every homemaker turns into a decorator, thinking up ideas for trimming her home in its most festive mood, in order to make it the one to be remembered for the taste and charm of its decorations and for the discrimination with which she has carried a co-ordinated theme throughout the house. Experience teaches how much decorations can contribute to the enjoyment of the festivities, and decorating should be a happy affair, with the whole family joining in this pleasurable task of the season.

Dried plants can be the star performers in all sorts of decorative Christmas ideas. There is a wealth of material in Nature's abundant supply if you look at it with an open mind. This type of material is versatile enough to fit into elaborate or restrained ideas, and it can be as festive as any other decorative material. Often it is far superior because of its inherent natural charm and marvelous lasting qualities. This latter is a boon to anyone who does not wish to have to replenish or freshen decorations during the holiday season. Decorations of dried plants are still as attractive the day they are removed as the day you put them in place for the holidays.

To fashion decorations from materials at hand instead of purchasing expensive commercial items requires a certain type of artistry. Imagination often counts for more than the work involved. But whatever you create has a personal touch, and with a store of dried plants there is no limit to the effects you can achieve. Give your imagination free reign and see what surprising things may result. And, to be practical, remember that there is nothing quite as satisfying as having decorations all in order *before* you are right in the middle of the scurry and bustle of Christmas.

The secret of success of any decoration is to have it coordinated to a home. Consider your style of furnishings before deciding upon an idea or a theme. The purpose of any decoration is to enrich, not to interfere. Is yours appropriate? Make it as elaborate or subdued as you wish, but key it to your home. What is right in one home can be out of place in another. There is nothing more grotesque than a highly stylized modern piece in a room of traditional furnishings.

When the furnishings of a home tend toward the Early American or are provincial in feeling, dried plant materials in their natural state seem the most compatible. Illustration 45, "Christmas Candle," is one way to add a contemporary

40 CONTEMPORARY ELEGANCE Formality is suggested by a mass design in a classic urn-shaped container. Symmetry is emphasized through a rhythmic pattern using comparatively identical materials on either side. Gourds, varying in size, shape, and texture are the major portion of the design material. A magnolia seed head, used at the top, and cones and chestnut burrs give textural contrast. Carrying the design over either side of the container are bunches of nuts, acorns, and paulownia pods. The design, including container, was sprayed first with silver and then with gold to give a richness of finish more elegant than that of one flat color.

41 TINSEL (*above right*) A contemporary interpretation relating the age-old cornucopia to our space age. A round board as a base positions the golden dowels to form triangular spaces and support the silver cornucopias. Each of these holds a small Styrofoam ball, silvered and lavishly glittered, surrounded by a frill of long-needle pine, dried, painted and glittered. The bow that ties the upper and lower areas of the design together is made of dried corn husks treated with gold and glitter.

twist to the use of natural cones. In another type of interior, possibly one with Adam or Georgian furnishings, a more dignified idea might be better, as shown in Illustration 40, "Contemporary Elegance." The modern approach, with its sparkle and glitter, seems to suit the modern interior, as shown in Illustration 41, "Tinsel."

LIVING ROOM

The living room is the most important place to use your artistry. It probably has a central feature that you will want to enrich. In a home of modern architecture, this might be a picture window or an area of open shelves. In the majority of contemporary homes, the mantel offers a splendid opportunity for a clever idea to become the center of attraction.

MANTEL IDEA

Each year my living-room mantel is cleared of its usual accessories to accommodate an appropriate Christmas idea. On one of the numerous shopping expeditions connected with Christmas, a pair of chubby little cupid wall brackets became the inspiration for Illustration 42, "On Cupid's Theme." A rectangular piece of lightweight plywood was painted off-

42 ON CUPID'S THEME A background of off-white puts in relief both the cupid brackets and the connecting garland of gold-sprayed dried plants. It includes seed pods of trumpet vine, eucalyptus, iris, and acorns with cups and nuts used separately. Chestnuts strung to simulate bunches of grapes, celosia, and leaves in the brackets. The small glasses holding votive candles were sprayed and sparkled. Photographed here against a plain background, the piece was originally used over a mantel.

white as a background for the gold and white cupids, which were attached at either end. Lightly-gilt-sprayed dried plants were glued to the plywood in a garland to join the brackets. Gold-toned velvet ribbon conceals the picture wire necessary to hang the piece above the mantel shelf. To repeat the theme, cupids, similar types of dried plants, and velvet ribbon were used in the decorative pieces on occasional and coffee tables. All of this is well suited to the color and mood of my furnishings.

Candles add a certain touch of glamour to a room that is also especially appropriate at Christmastime. The easiest way to avoid a fire hazard when using candles with dried plants is to protect the candles in some way. Votive candles in small inexpensive glasses are the simplest to use and yet are perfectly safe when the candles are lit. Such glasses are obtainable at very small cost and can be colored or ornamented to harmonize with any decorative idea. A series of these candles, as seen in Illustration 42, "On Cupid's Theme," is most effective as the small candle flames glow and flicker all about the room.

HANGING DECORATION

A traditional idea is to use a hanging decoration, and it can be adapted to the present so that it becomes entirely contemporary. With a little imagination and a different handling of decorative material, original effects are easily created for doorway, hall, picture or bay window, or any other place which at this season needs some kind of ornamentation. Each piece should be designed for a specific place if it is to give the maximum effect.

43

GLAMOROUS BALL A sparkling hanging decoration made on a large Styrofoam ball. The covering includes cones of several sizes, seed pods, small flowers, foliages, and various other bits of dried plants. The brightly colored angels and dwarfs are package-wrap figures and the red sequins, used in groups, stand out against the gold-sprayed dried plants.

Long before Christmas, the foundation of a hanging decoration, shown in Illustration 43, "Glamorous Ball," was started. A large Styrofoam ball, about nine inches in diameter, was threaded through its center with a half-inch braid. The braid was made of many strands of gold metallic thread such as one would use in crocheting. The ends were purposely exposed at the bottom of the ball to be a finishing tassel. When suspended by this braid, the ball was easy to cover and provided an excellent opportunity to use all of those queer little treasures of dried plants which had been kept for some as-yet-unthought-of use.

Important points to remember in selecting materials to cover a ball of this nature are size for good proportion on the ball and variety in shape and texture for over-all surface interest. All of the material should be worked into the ball so that its shape is retained and no material protrudes to spoil the roundness. The technique for inserting the material is similar to that described for the ball topiary in Chapter 6. Once the ball was completely covered, the entire covering was lightly sprayed with gold, and gay little figures and the largest red sequins that could be purchased were added. The figures provide the flash of color and the sequins sparkle as the ball sways on its golden braid. If you went to purchase such a decorative piece, you would surely find that it had a very fancy price tag.

WHITE CHRISTMAS THEME

White Christmas is always an appropriate theme for a decoration. It is sparkling, festive, and suggestive of the season. Dried plants can be easily adapted to this theme of white, which can be made to harmonize with any type of room, traditional or modern. White decorations could be a decided complement to a room in brilliant color or could supply the light touch to furnishings that are dark.

Stunning effects can result from lightly spraying dried plants with dull-white paint or glamorizing them with a light application of artificial snow. "Winter White," Illustration 44, uses this idea to convert a branch and some ordinary dried plants into a distinctive decorative piece. A hollow tree branch, with a delightful curve, inspired the idea. You hardly recognize the roadside mullein in its dress of winter frost. The round forms represent snowballs tumbling down a hill. The mood is further carried out by the small white ceramic birds. This is but one of endless possible ideas for decorative pieces on the winter white theme.

WINTER WHITE *(see Frontispiece)* A branch screwed to a piece of plywood is the basis of the composition. Stalks of mullein (wild verbascum) are used at top and bottom to accentuate the shape of the branch by lengthening its curving silhouette; mahonia leaves add interest to the curve. For a change of form, small Styrofoam balls act as a base for various dried plants such as cones of sequoia, alder, pods of iris, poppy, dictamnus (gas-plant). Two white ceramic birds fit the theme of the all-white composition.

CONES

Many of the needle evergreens, known as conifers, produce the most fascinating structures to protect and dispel their seeds. We speak of these generally as cones. When you compare a few cones you will realize how varied are the sizes and how lovely are the shapes and colors which Nature gives these seed formations. They are still a great favorite as a decorative material, yet we can give the traditional cone a new individual appearance by a different handling.

The rich natural color tones in these wood structures are highly ornamental. Though the values of brown do predominate, there is wide variation from the light tan of a Sitka spruce cone to the mahogany of a Douglas fir. The cones of piñon pine are delightful, with their attractive shape, size, and natural color. The scales of some seem to have been sprayed with small areas of yellow and those of others with chartreuse. You cannot find a more versatile dried plant material than cones if you are of the school of thought that prefers natural material for decorations. Cones are entirely satisfactory to be used as the only material for an idea, yet they also combine wonderfully with other materials.

A free-standing decoration of cones has many possible uses and can be either large or small, according to the idea and the size of the cones. A simple grouping about a large candle shows off the cones' natural charm and color. Such groupings can have many variations and can be made with one or several kinds of cones, as shown in Illustration 45, "Christmas Candle." The candle was made especially for the design, as none of an appropriate size or color could be purchased. A modern clear-glass cylinder protects the cones from the candle flame.

45
CHRISTMAS CANDLE A Styrofoam circle, 10″ diameter, covered with gold foil is the base to hold the 11″-tall homemade brown candle in a 12″-high clear glass cylinder. The surrounding group of cones includes those of Scotch, white, ponderosa, and pinyon pine, cedar, and Douglas fir. A series of sweet-gum balls (liquid-amber) is introduced for added variety.

KITCHEN DECORATION

Your kitchen should be made as festive as the rest of your home, to supply pleasant surroundings while you prepare the season's special menus. Do not overlook the wonderful opportunities for a novel decoration in your kitchen. What is more appropriate than to develop a decorative piece from kitchen items? Would you dream that such a distinctive epergne could be created from funnels and a cake tin? "Funnels for Fun," Illustration 47, demonstrates what an interesting piece can be fashioned. In fact, you may be interested in using it elsewhere.

Once the funnel construction is complete—it is done on a central dowel stick—it is a simple matter to position the dried plants. Gold was the right note for my yellow kitchen, but color can easily be added to this type of decorative piece by including a few colored tree ornaments. This is but one idea. Look about your kitchen for an inspiration, and this year plan something interesting. It will really be fun.

COLORING DRIED PLANTS FOR DECORATIONS

A wealth of dried plants is far more effective for certain types of Christmas decorations when the plants are given coloring or finish of some kind. Wonderful results can be achieved with paint, artificial snow, glitter, and sprinkle if these are used with discretion and applied intelligently. The freedom in the present trend of designing allows you to branch out in new directions in your decorations. Anything is possible, provided you keep within the bounds of good taste and common sense. Illustration 41, "Tinsel," in a modern manner, and

FUNNEL FOR FUN

CONSTRUCTION: An 18″ dowel, anchored to the center of a 9″ round cake tin with a thin block of wood, supports three tin funnels of graduated sizes. To form the epergne, each one is positioned on the dowel with glue. Notice how the design is started in the top funnel, and how the bunched chestnuts are placed to start rhythm and balance that will be felt in the completed design.

Illustration 40, "Traditional Elegance," in a traditional manner, both have various finishes applied to all their design materials.

Before you apply any treatment to dried plants for decorative purposes, always be certain that the plants are dry and free of dust or loose particles or your finish may be impaired. This applies particularly when using white. It is practical to do most of the construction of an idea before the finish is applied, and the easiest way to paint or gild is with a spray can, leaving no brushes to clean. But never cover the plants to the point that natural form and charm are lost. A light application is ample, especially when using a metallic paint. Leaves need be coated only on the upper surface. If you wish sparkle or glitter to adhere, sprinkle lavishly while the paint is wet.

NUMBER, SIZE, AND COLOR OF DECORATIONS

Questions are repeatedly asked about Christmas decorations. Possibly there are answers to yours in the following:

How many decorations in a room?

In an average-size room, three or possibly four appropriately placed decorative units are ample. Although Christmas calls for a lavish decorative effect, the plan must be controlled. Too many decorative pieces will cause a cluttered look; too few may leave your decorative scheme looking unfinished. The idea is to have decorations enrich a room, not smother it.

47

FUNNEL FOR FUN An idea for the kitchen. Wheat, dock, small cones, and seed pods fill the top funnel. The placement of strung chestnuts in the middle and lower funnels provides rhythm to carry the eye through the design. The design materials, all previously gilded and sparkled, include acorns, cones of several kinds, and foliage. The cake tin at the bottom has artichokes, sweet-gum balls, cones, and foliage. Small gold Christmas-tree balls were grouped throughout for their contrasting mirror-smooth sparkle.

What size for a decoration?

There is an ideal size for each decoration placed in a room. This size contributes to or destroys the effect. When a decoration is too small, it is ineffective; conversely, when it is too large, it dominates. For example, the dimensions of a decorative piece planned for a coffee or end table would be smaller than those of one planned for a console or occasional table. A mantel would require something in a larger size to be effective from all parts of a room.

What color shall Christmas decorations be?

The present trend is to use gay, festive colors but to key them to the decor of the room. It is no longer necessary to feel restricted to the traditional association of red and green. None of the Christmas spirit is lost by the use of various colors. We see stunning effects with pink, blue, chartreuse, and lavender. Gold and silver are extremely popular. Begin with the color of your room and plan from there.

In the final analysis it is not how many decorations you use nor how lavish they may be but how well you have planned that brings the festive mood to your home. Decorations are both symbols of the hospitality that creates the holiday atmosphere and the ingredients of the generous spirit that makes the season of Christmas a wonderful experience. There are endless ways to dress your home in its most attractive attire. It is the sense of fitness in creative decorating that leaves the glowing picture in the memories of the family who lives in the home and of the friends who visit it at the holiday season.

POINTS TO BE CONSIDERED IN CHRISTMAS DECORATIONS:

1. Key the style of all decorations to the home in which they are to be used.

2. Make decorations in gay and festive colors related to those already in the rooms.

3. Be practical by choosing materials with lasting qualities.

4. Use materials available at little cost.

5. Plan and start far in advance.

And enjoy the preparation of your decorations!

Chapter Eight

Sources of Plants to Dry

Where do you find plants suitable for drying? Everywhere—for the world of Nature, with its infinite variety, is full of wonderful things, if you are alert and willing to see them. The supply is endless, and each season brings new possibilities to challenge your drying ability.

With the recent trend toward wider use of dried materials, many plants never before considered as suitable for drying have been used with great success. You may really become excited when you discover how well many of the familiar plants in your own area can be dried. They may be entirely different from the plants in my area, but if they can be used for your decorative purposes, does it really matter what kind they are?

YOUR GARDEN AS A SOURCE

In any part of our country, much of the joy of a contemporary suburban home is the space it affords for a garden in which to grow the plants you like. But have you realized that your own garden is one of the very best sources of plants for drying? Many of your favorite flowers may be preserved, and there are many interesting forms of foliage to be found in a garden. Your garden may have still other equally attractive items, such as seed pods, branches, and vine tendrils. Any garden has wonderful possibilities for drying, and even the smallest one offers an ample supply.

There are many advantages to using your own garden as a source of drying material. (My small garden has proved to be a most rewarding source.) You are assured of a continuing supply, and during the growing season you can watch the development of the plants. You can cut the plants when they are at exactly the right stage for drying, when a bloom is at its prime beauty or when a plant is at an interesting stage in its development. Your material for drying is fresh and can be processed immediately. You are saved the time and trouble of searching for it, as it is at your very doorstep. Another advantage is that you can grow the plants you prefer in the colors which dominate the decor of your home.

Unless you have an extensive garden and professional assistance, it is difficult to attempt an enormous variety; but do plan a border or planting with an interesting even if limited choice. If the garden is small, flowers can still serve the dual purpose of being enjoyed for both garden color and drying material, for the few picked here and there for drying will never be missed. It is fun to experiment with growing and drying new kinds each year and, in this way, to acquire experience in growing as well as variety in your dried-plant supply for artistic uses.

Flowers are one of the most fascinating of all materials for drying because of their glorious colors and forms. If you start in spring, no matter where you live, you can find an ample supply of interesting flowers to be dried all through the growing season, from bulbs to chrysanthemums.

SPRING BULBS

Have you ever thought of drying a few of the flowers from your spring bulbs to be used with the interesting lines of pussy willow? Such a combination will make a delightful springtime dried arrangement. Such bulbs as narcissus, daffodil, and tulip are often included in a border planting, and any of their blossoms can be dried to preserve their beautiful color and form.

ROSES

The trellis or fence in your back yard may have a climbing rose or your border may include hybrid teas or florabundas. At their abundance of bloom, pick and dry a few of these engaging flowers. Good results have been achieved with many varieties of roses, and those of a clear pink, rose, or red remain true to color. Rose foliage is best dried separately and combined with the flowers when they are arranged.

PEONIES

Peonies are a favorite in many border plantings. If yours has some of the single or the Japanese types, do not overlook them as subjects for drying. Several are a glorious addition to many types of dried arrangements. They retain an excellent form and color, particularly the pink ones with golden centers. The leaves of peonies are excellent for drying, either in spring or in fall, when you tidy the garden for winter.

SPIKE FORMS

Taller types of plants are usually used in a border or at the back of a bed for height. Larkspur, delphinium, and stock are all wonderful for drying. They also keep good form and color, especially the deep-blue and purple ones. Snapdragons are easy to dry, as is liatris.

HYDRANGEA

Large showy clusters of hydrangea are seen in many gardens. The lovely blue, pink, and lavender ones will retain their color if they are picked in an early stage of bloom. *Note:* This principle of drying applies to practically all flowers in which you wish to retain good color. On the woody-stemmed hydrangeas, the white pointed clusters of small flowers dry satisfactorily, and if you leave some on the plant until they turn a rusty pink in fall, you have still another color for arrangements.

EVERLASTINGS

The so-called everlastings have a place in many gardens. This family of plants includes many kinds, and their papery-textured flowers are among the best subjects for drying. Statice, with tiny flowers on long stems, grows in many colors and dries easily and quickly. Strawflowers have been famous as a dried material for many years. *Note:* For the best results, pick either of these when the flowers are only one quarter to one half open, since they open further during the drying. Globe amaranth is another plant with a papery texture in its clover-shaped flower heads.

ANNUALS

Annuals are included in practically all gardens for their quick floral results. The universal favorites seem to be marigold and zinnia. At the height of their bloom, you can easily cut some for drying without spoiling the color effect in the garden. Marigolds have two main classifications: small-flowered ones termed "French" and the large-flowered "African." The larger types are the best for drying. Excellent results have been obtained with both the newer pale-yellow ones, Climax, and the old favorite, Guinea Gold. The same principle applies to drying zinnias, with the larger types of giant, cactus, and dahlia proving to be better as subjects for drying than the lilliput types.

CELOSIA

Celosia (cockscomb), a fascinating garden plant, is a great favorite for fall color in a garden. Modern methods of hybridizing have given many new rich colors to this old-time flower. Today there are two types: feathery plumes and stiff fluted crests. Both types can be dried, but I have found the crest type the most rewarding. *Note:* Gather these when color is rich and clear, never past its prime, and before the little black seeds begin to drop.

DAHLIAS AND CHRYSANTHEMUMS

Dahlias and chrysanthemums seem to be flowers that gardeners make a specialty of, and an enthusiastic person will devote a special space to her favorite. If you have space for only a few of these plants, choose those of the smaller sizes for the best results in drying the flowers.

FOLIAGE AS A SOURCE OF MATERIALS TO DRY

Many of the plants in a foundation planting are ideal for drying. Have you ever thought of drying a branch of leucothoë, rhododendron, andromeda, viburnum, magnolia, or mahonia, to mention just a few? Their foliage dries well, especially that of magnolia and viburnum. Cherry laurel, widely used in the South, and salal, commonly called lemon, of the Pacific Coast are excellent for drying. You may find other equally suitable ones in your planting.

We see the trees in our neighborhood every day, but we take them so for granted that we entirely forget that they offer a wealth of interesting material to be dried for many decorative uses. Many of the well-known trees—such as maple, oak, beech, poplar, and gum—thrive in various sections of the country, and these can provide distinctive green foliage in spring and colorful leaves in fall, either of which are entirely adaptable to drying. Other sections of the country have their native trees, such as California's big-leaf maple and eucalyptus, Carolina's magnolia, and Florida's palm. Each has a distinguished quality when it is dried.

Garden plants are a source of interesting leaves for drying. There are many shapes, such as the pointed leaves of iris, gladiolus, and yucca. Hosta (funkia) has an oval-shaped leaf that dries beautifully. Artemisia offers many delightful forms to be dried, especially the smoky gray of silver king. Canna, a well-known garden plant, has lovely large leaves with strong bold form that can be used in modern design, and either the green or the brown can be dried.

VARIOUS GARDEN SOURCES OF DRYING MATERIAL

Your garden can supply other attractive items for drying besides flowers and foliages. For example, there are the round blue-gray heads of echinops (globe thistle), the cup shapes of the Oriental poppy seedcases, the stems of dictamnus (gas plant) and baptisia (false indigo), and the bright-orange balloon seedcases of the Chinese lantern plant. Perennial sweetpea, trumpet, and wisteria vines develop most interesting seed pods for drying.

In spring, a wisteria is delightful with its exquisite perfume, but unfortunately the tresses do not seem to dry well. However, the vine tendrils can supply some of the most fascinating dried material if you accentuate the natural twist or curl before drying. Euonymus has a most interesting bark on its branches, and many other vines can supply just such material for drying if you are willing to seek them out.

FRUITS AND VEGETABLES

The fruit and vegetable bins of a market are another source of drying materials. You will have fun experimenting in this area because when this type of plant material is dry it provides individual forms and colors and interesting textures that have a certain distinction all their own. Since they are not usually considered as suited to drying, these materials will cause comment.

These materials can be purchased at any time of the year. Such vegetables as artichokes, mushrooms, and peppers and such fruits as lemon and lime are prevalent at all seasons. Pomegranate and okra may be seasonal. Peas and beans are other items of interest. In the selection of such materials for drying, it is preferable to choose those that are underripe, never overripe, and free of blemish, bruise, or mark.

Globe artichoke, with its edible flower head, is really handsome if the petallike scales are opened before it is dried. Try mushrooms and peppers for interesting textures and shapes. Ornamental corn has been known for years as a dried material, and it is still an excellent colorful design element. The possibilities for artistic uses of various other parts of the corn plant are fully described in *Handbook of Dried Arrangements and Decorations.*

A vegetable garden is another source of material to be dried. The seed clusters of leek and onion assume fascinating curved lines while drying. The dried leaves of flowering kale, beet, and horse-radish are unusual touches for a design. The herbs in a vegetable garden can also be a source of drying material, as can the flower stalks of rhubarb.

WILD PLANTS

On a trip into the country, there are always wonderful things to be discovered along the roadside and in fields, woods, and meadows. Each area of our country has its native plants. People may term some of them weeds, but they are a wonderful source of interesting material. If you are observant, you will see that Nature gives each plant a distinct character for the conditions in which it must grow.

Wild grasses are but one example of such distinct character. Marsh grasses are tall, strong, and stately in their environment, in contrast to the dainty, lacy-headed field grasses. Interesting seed pods and cases appear on wild plants, and each is ingeniously constructed to fulfill its purpose. Mullein (wild verbascum), with stalks often growing to six feet, is a common sight along many roadside banks: one or two of these can be extremely useful in decorative work. Dock, called sorrel, is another common weed: the small clusters of green flowers which appear on its long stems are not attractive until they turn copper-colored or a leathery tan, but then they are a marvelous contrast to orange or pink dried plants.

Teasel is another of the interesting wild plants. Its coarse, prickly, thistlelike heads are most distinctive and are sometimes grown as garden ornamentals. Sumac has dense fruit heads, and those of the staghorn variety will retain their deep, rich, red, velvety appearance when dry.

Wild flowers give color to the landscape all during spring and summer. We see the dusty rose of joe-pye weed, the brilliant-yellow splotches of goldenrod and tansy, and the cheerful red of Oswego tea. In many areas Queen Anne's lace is abundant, with its filmy, snowy-white flowers covering the fields. Anyone who has seen the lupine or delphinium covering the fields of the West Coast will not soon forget it.

CONSERVATION

You may be surprised at the suggestion to gather wild plants with so much emphasis being placed on conservation today. But many wild plants do grow so abundantly that, if you are selective, no one should object to your gathering a few. Certain plants are on a restricted list in each area, and this protection is to avoid their extermination. You should contact the local authorities and learn the ones that are protected by the conservation list in your area.

When you are gathering plants for drying from the wild, always exercise the same care you would in cutting a plant from your own garden. Pick in moderation, no more than you can use, and never destroy a wild plant.

COMMERCIAL SOURCES

Anyone who lives in the city and does not have the advantages of a garden must depend upon the neighborhood florist to fill her needs for plants. With the present popularity of dried plants for decoration, the alert florist stocks a small supply of dried plants for the convenience of his customers, but he can obtain specialty items from his supplier.

At the florist's, if you are attracted by the fresh bold leaves of some tropical plant—such as ti, dracaena, anthurium, or strelitzia—these can easily be dried, like any other foliage. Cycas, large-leaf philodendron, and croton are other tropical foliages to be obtained at the florist's.

In this jet age, the demand created by the trend to dried plants can be filled. Firms in all parts of the country and the world ship their dried-plant specialities to our markets. One can find many kinds at all times of the year. It is not unusual to see wood roses from Hawaii; Jeffrey, digger, and piñon cones from the Pacific Coast; and palms from Florida displayed at the same counter of a shop. The sight of such a display should inspire one to arrange dried plants, for a purchase is ready for immediate use.

Today dried plants are obtainable by mail order, and advertisements of such products are found in garden and women's magazines. However, there is one disadvantage to this source. If you do not have some knowledge of what the dried plant is like, you may be completely surprised when your purchase arrives. When a catalog lists parts of a plant—such as palm spathe, calyx, or boot or pods of datura or tornillo—do you know what each looks like? Are you tempted to find out? The surprise may be a pleasant one. On the several occasions when I have been tempted, some of the most interesting things have come.

SUMMARY OF SOURCES

1. Every garden has many possibilities—trees, shrubs, annuals, perennials, vines, bulbs, etc.—of materials to be dried.

2. Fruits and vegetables are a source for certain kinds of decorative forms.

3. Wild plants are a source of distinctive materials, if conservation restrictions are observed.

4. The florist is a convenient source, with already-dried materials available, too.

5. Mail order is a source, with various areas specializing in their native plants, available already dried.

Chapter Nine

Summary of Ways to Dry Plants

What is the best way to dry plants? Is there a rule for drying plants? These are the most frequently asked questions. There is no one way, rule, or formula that can be applied to the drying of all plants. However, there are basic procedures that apply to drying, and when used with common sense they will produce most satisfying results.

The first thing is to become conscious of the infinite differences in plant forms, structures, tissues, and textures and the plants' rates of transpiration. These factors vary greatly in flowers, foliages, and other plant materials to be dried for artistic uses. Each has some bearing on drying results. For example, all plants do not dry in the same period of time, as moisture retention is far greater in some than in others. A flower's texture and number of petals have direct bearings on the time of drying.

Climate is also a factor in drying, for if it is moist, with high humidity, more care must be taken in the selection and drying of plants than if conditions are clear and dry. Because we have learned to be conscious of these factors and to take them into consideration, we are able to dry a greater variety of plants for our contemporary artistic uses.

The principle involved in the drying of all plants is to withdraw the juice, sap, or moisture from the plant to make it last indefinitely. The details of this principle were fully discussed in my former books, *The Art of Drying Plants and Flowers* and *A Handbook of Dried Arrangements and Decorations.*

The following summarizes the general procedures for drying plants, and they can be adapted to suit various materials and conditions.

GENERAL PROCEDURE TO SERVE AS A GUIDE FOR DRYING FLOWERS

1. Choose flowers of good color and quality that are fresh and crisp. Inferior ones give inferior results.

2. Cut flowers when they have the least surface moisture on parts or petals.

3. Flowers one-third to one-half open are at the best stage.

4. A stem of six to eight inches is adequate.

5. Strip all unnecessary foliage from stem. Stem may also be stripped bare and foliage dried separately.

6. Methods of drying flowers:

Air Drying—Hang upside down, singly or in small groups, in a warm place with circulation of air. Fasten securely, as stems shrink when drying. One to two weeks' drying time.

Agent Drying—Bury flowers in a dry mixture (agent) in a container (cardboard or wax-coated).

Agent mixture is one-half corn meal and one-half borax. To each quart add three tablespoons of salt.

Completely cover flower; leave stem exposed and container uncovered during drying.

Time of drying depends on structure of flower—eight to fifteen days. Remove flower by gradually pouring off mixture; brush gently with soft artist's brush if specks remain.

7. Store dried flowers in a covered box until used.

The drying of flowers can be as simple or as complicated as you wish to make it. The easiest of all methods is air drying by hanging the flowers upside down. However, the types suited to this method are somewhat limited and not all flowers can be dried successfully this way. Air drying is excellent for the finer and thinner types, such as babies'-breath and the papery-tissued flowers such as strawflower and statice. Flowers that have a dense head of fleshy petals do not retain their dimensional form if dried by this method.

The agent method is applicable to a far wider range of flowers, although it does take a bit more time and effort. This method retains the natural colors of flowers and also their dimensional forms, both of which are essential if the flowers are to be used for decorative purposes. You can start with daffodils in spring and continue through summer flowers and then go on to the chrysanthemums of fall.

Many years of investigation of different substances as drying agents for the so-called tenderer types of flowers have been carried on in search of the best one. It is evident from the trials and tests of hundreds of specimens with numerous agents, used in various ways and on many types of flowers, that a combination of substances is far superior to one alone. These experiments have demonstrated that my mixture is as foolproof as any and that its performance far exceeds that of others, including the newer chemical substances. Its ingredients, given in the preceding summary, are inexpensive and easily available and can be reused time and time again with no new treatment of any kind. Flowers dried in this way remain in good condition for several years and will even travel many miles for lecture demonstrations.

SHORT LIST OF FLOWERS TO BE DRIED BY HANGING UPSIDE DOWN

Amaranth
Belles of Ireland
Celosia (cockscomb)
Goldenrod
Joe-pye weed
Statice
Strawflower
Yarrow

SHORT LIST OF FLOWERS TO BE DRIED BY AGENT METHOD

Daffodil
Delphinium
Hydrangea
Larkspur
Marigold
Peony
Rose
Zinnia

GENERAL PROCEDURE TO SERVE AS A GUIDE FOR DRYING FOLIAGE

1. Choose only leaves of good color, quality, texture, and substance.

2. Cut leaves when they have the least surface moisture.

3. Process large leaves singly or leaved branches twelve to fourteen inches long.

4. Methods of drying foliage:

Air Drying—Hang a large leaf or branch singly, upside down, in a warm dry place with circulation of air. One to two weeks' drying time.

Or, lay leaf or leaved branch on absorbent paper in a warm dry place with circulation of air. One to two weeks' drying time. Turn over twice during drying to give leaf a pleasing shape.

Pressing—Place foliage between folds of absorbent paper with even weight on top. Two to four weeks' drying time.

Absorption—Suitable method for large leaves or leaved branch not exceeding twenty inches. Slash or mash end of stem for three inches. Stand in tall container. Add mixture of one part glycerine to two parts water to a depth of six inches. Keep in warm dry place. Absorption period, two to four weeks. Absorption is complete when solution reaches all parts; this is easily visible.

5. Store foliage in covered box until used.

The method you select for the drying of foliage will depend upon the way in which you propose to use the foliage in a design idea. Each of the above methods gives a different result. For example, leaves processed by pressing will become flat, with no dimensional quality and often paper thin. Those done by either method of air drying will take on fantastic shapes as the air dries the various parts. (Try some this way and you will be intrigued by the shapes the leaves assume.)

The absorption method for keeping foliage is becoming more popular now that it is better known. Foliage cured in this way has many advantages. It will remain entirely flexible and does not become stiff as in other methods. Some of my leaves are several years old and are still entirely usable. There is only one objection: the natural color of the foliage is lost, though the brown tone that develops is a rich warm one entirely suited to use with other dried plants. In fact, the mahogany tone is stunning with such colors as the pink of dried peonies and the blue of dried hydrangeas. But not every kind of foliage will respond to this method.

SHORT LIST OF FOLIAGE TO BE PROCESSED BY ABSORPTION METHOD

Aspidistra	Leucothoe
Dracaena	Magnolia
Eucalyptus	Mahonia
Lemon (Salal)	Peony

Viburnum (especially leather-leaf)

GENERAL PROCEDURE TO SERVE AS A GUIDE FOR DRYING FRUITS AND VEGETABLES

1. Choose only fruits or vegetables free of marks and blemishes.

2. Clean skin of any dirt or dust.

3. Air-dry fruits and vegetables.

4. Place stemless fruits or vegetables on raised, perforated surface for free circulation of air to all parts. Place in cool, dry location and turn several times during drying.

5. Hang stemmed fruits or vegetables in cool dry spot with circulation of air.

6. Drying time varies with size from three weeks to three months.

From the many varieties of fruits and vegetables, only a limited number have proven amenable to good drying and retention of form and color. Fruits and vegetables, because of their fleshy nature and high moisture content, take longer to dry than other types of plant material. This applies especially to fruits. In the first week they will appear soft and useless, but as moisture evaporates they will turn hard and firm. Pomegranates may take as long as three months to become completely dry.

SHORT LIST OF FRUITS AND VEGETABLES FOR DRYING

Kumquat	Artichoke
Lemon	Mushroom
Lime	Okra
Pomegranate	Pepper

Seed stems of leek and onion

SUMMARY OF EQUIPMENT NEEDED FOR DRYING PLANTS

You will need the following:

For cutting—scissors, clippers, knife.

For upside-down drying of flowers, foliage, etc.—Twistems, elastics, or something similar to hold material securely in place.

For agent method of drying flowers—borax, corn meal, and salt for agent mixture. Spoon, box (cardboard, wax-coated, or plastic), artist's brush, jars to store agent.

For processing of foliage—glycerine, water, tall container.

For foliage pressing—absorbent paper and weights.

For fruit and vegetable drying—raised perforated surface.

For mechanics of securing, lengthening, and supporting stems—corsage tape, wire, pipe cleaners, florist's sticks, Twistems, elastics, raffia.

For mechanics to secure plants in container—Styrofoam, clay, needle holder.

Optional items—toothpicks, pins, hollow stems (dried).

Index